Sleep Smarter Unlocking the Secrets to Optimal Sleep and Performance

Adeeba

Sleep Smarter Unlocking the Secrets to Optimal Sleep and Performance

Copyright © 2023 by Adeeba

The first edition was published in 2023

ISBN:
Published by:
Sunshine
1663 Liberty Drive
Hyderabad, IN 47403
www.Sunshinepublishers.com

This book is self-published using on-demand printing and publishing, which allows it to be printed and distributed globally

TABLE OF CONTENT

Chapter 6: Conclusion: Embracing the Power of Sleep   00

Chapter 1: The Importance of Optimal Sleep

Understanding the Power of Sleep

Sleep is a fundamental aspect of our lives, yet it is often overlooked and undervalued. In the modern world, where productivity and achievement are prioritized, sleep tends to take a backseat. However, the power of sleep cannot be underestimated. In this subchapter, we will delve into the many ways sleep can greatly impact our overall well-being and performance.

One of the key aspects of understanding the power of sleep lies in its ability to restore and rejuvenate our bodies. During sleep, our bodies undergo essential processes that promote healing, repair damaged cells, and strengthen our immune system. Lack of sleep, on the other hand, can leave us susceptible to illnesses, hinder recovery, and compromise our overall health.

Moreover, sleep plays a crucial role in cognitive functions such as memory, attention, and learning. Adequate sleep allows our brains to consolidate and organize information acquired throughout the day, leading to improved memory retention and recall. On the contrary, insufficient sleep can impair cognitive abilities, negatively impacting our performance in various areas of life.

The power of sleep also extends to our emotional well-being. A good night's sleep can enhance our mood, resilience, and overall emotional stability. Conversely, chronic sleep deprivation is often associated with increased levels of stress, anxiety, and mood disorders. Getting enough sleep can significantly contribute to our mental and emotional health, allowing us to navigate life's challenges with greater ease.

Additionally, sleep has a profound impact on our physical appearance. Lack of sleep can lead to dark circles under the eyes, dull skin, and premature aging. On the contrary, quality sleep can promote healthy skin, reduce the appearance of wrinkles, and give us a vibrant, refreshed look.

Understanding the power of sleep is not just about recognizing its benefits but also about adopting healthy sleep habits. This subchapter will provide practical tips and strategies for optimizing your sleep, such as establishing a consistent sleep schedule, creating a sleep-friendly environment, and implementing relaxation techniques before bed.

In conclusion, sleep is not just a mere state of unconsciousness; it is a powerful force that influences every aspect of our lives. By understanding and harnessing the power of sleep, we can unlock optimal sleep and performance, leading to improved physical health, cognitive abilities, emotional well-being, and overall quality of life. It's time to prioritize sleep and reap the countless benefits it offers.

The science behind sleep

In the fast-paced world we live in, sleep often takes a backseat to our busy schedules and endless to-do lists. However, understanding the science behind sleep can help us realize the immense power it holds in optimizing our performance and overall well-being.

Sleep is not just a state of rest; it is a complex biological process that involves numerous intricate mechanisms. Our bodies and brains undergo a series of essential functions during sleep, allowing us to wake up refreshed and ready to tackle the day ahead.

One of the key aspects of sleep is its role in memory consolidation. During sleep, our brains process and store information, helping us retain new knowledge and experiences. Studies have shown that a good night's sleep can significantly enhance both learning and problem-solving abilities. In fact, getting sufficient sleep has been linked to improved academic performance, creativity, and critical thinking skills.

Sleep also plays a vital role in regulating our emotions. Lack of sleep can lead to increased irritability, mood swings, and even depression. During sleep, our brains reset and restore emotional balance, ensuring that we wake up with a more stable and positive mindset.

Furthermore, sleep is closely intertwined with our physical health. It is during sleep that our bodies repair and rejuvenate themselves. Adequate sleep has been linked to a strengthened immune system, better cardiovascular health, and a reduced risk of chronic diseases such as diabetes and obesity. Additionally, sleep is crucial for athletic performance, as it aids in muscle recovery and growth.

Understanding the science behind sleep can also shed light on the importance of quality sleep. It is not just about the number of hours we spend in bed; the quality of our sleep matters too. Factors such as sleep environment, sleep hygiene, and the sleep-wake cycle all play a crucial role in ensuring we achieve optimal sleep.

In conclusion, sleep is not just a luxury; it is a fundamental necessity for our physical, mental, and emotional well-being. By understanding the science behind sleep, we can unlock its immense power and use it to enhance our performance in all aspects of life. So, let's prioritize sleep and reap the countless benefits it has to offer.

Different stages of sleep

Understanding the different stages of sleep is crucial to optimizing our sleep quality and overall performance. Sleep is not a uniform state; instead, it consists of several distinct stages that occur in a cyclical pattern throughout the night. In this subchapter, we will delve into the fascinating world of sleep stages and explore their significance in harnessing the power of sleep for optimal performance.

The sleep cycle can be divided into two main categories: non-rapid eye movement (NREM) sleep and rapid eye movement (REM) sleep. NREM sleep can be further categorized into three stages: N1, N2, and N3, while REM sleep represents the fifth stage.

During the initial stage, N1, we experience a transition from wakefulness to sleep. This stage is characterized by light sleep, and it is relatively easy to wake up from this stage. As we progress into the next stage, N2, our brain waves slow down, and our body temperature drops. This stage is crucial for memory consolidation and learning.

The third stage, N3, is often referred to as deep sleep or slow-wave sleep. This is the stage where our body repairs and rejuvenates itself. Growth hormone is released, muscle tissue is repaired, and our immune system is strengthened. Deep sleep is essential for physical recovery and plays a critical role in maintaining overall health.

After completing the NREM sleep stages, we enter REM sleep. This stage is characterized by rapid eye movements and vivid dreaming. REM sleep is crucial for cognitive function, memory consolidation, and emotional regulation. It is during this stage that our brain processes and stores information, helping us learn and adapt to new experiences.

The sleep cycle typically lasts around 90 minutes, and we go through several cycles each night. While NREM sleep predominates in the earlier part of the night, REM sleep becomes more prominent in the later cycles. A healthy sleep pattern includes an adequate amount of each stage, ensuring that we reap the benefits of both physical and mental restoration.

Understanding the different stages of sleep empowers us to optimize our sleep habits for improved performance. By prioritizing a consistent sleep schedule, creating a sleep-friendly environment, and adopting relaxation techniques, we can enhance the quality and duration of each sleep stage. The power of sleep lies in its ability to restore, rejuvenate, and optimize our physical and mental well-being. By unlocking the secrets of the sleep stages, we can harness this power to achieve peak performance in all areas of our lives.

The role of sleep in physical and mental health

The role of sleep in physical and mental health is a crucial aspect of our overall well-being. In the hustle and bustle of our modern lives, we often overlook the importance of quality sleep. However, in the book "Sleep Smarter: Unlocking the Secrets to Optimal Sleep and Performance," we delve into the power of sleep and how it affects various aspects of our lives.

To begin with, let's explore the physical health benefits of adequate sleep. During sleep, our body goes into repair and restoration mode. It is during this time that our muscles recover from the day's activities, and our immune system strengthens, helping to ward off illnesses and diseases. Furthermore, research shows that a lack of sleep can lead to weight gain and obesity due to disrupted hormone levels, particularly those that regulate appetite. By prioritizing sleep, we can maintain a healthy weight and reduce the risk of chronic diseases such as diabetes and heart disease.

In addition to physical health, sleep also plays a vital role in our mental well-being. When we sleep, our brain consolidates and organizes information, helping us retain memories and improve learning and cognitive function. Lack of sleep, on the other hand, can lead to cognitive impairments, difficulty concentrating, and decreased productivity. Moreover, sleep deprivation is closely linked to mental health disorders such as depression and anxiety. By making sleep a priority, we can improve our mood, reduce stress levels, and enhance our overall mental resilience.

Understanding the power of sleep is essential for optimizing our performance in all areas of life. Whether you are an athlete striving for peak physical performance or an individual seeking to excel in your professional and personal life, sleep is the secret weapon you need. By ensuring you get enough quality sleep, you can enhance your athletic performance, increase your focus and productivity, and improve your decision-making abilities.

In conclusion, sleep is not just a luxury; it is a fundamental pillar of our physical and mental health. By recognizing the role of sleep in our overall well-being, we can harness its power to unlock our full potential. So, make sleep a priority, create a sleep-friendly environment, and establish a consistent sleep routine. The benefits of optimal sleep are endless, and by implementing the strategies outlined in "Sleep Smarter: Unlocking the Secrets to Optimal Sleep and Performance," you can experience a transformative shift in your life.

Sleep Deprivation and its Consequences

In today's fast-paced world, sleep deprivation has become a common problem affecting people of all ages and backgrounds. In this subchapter, we will explore the detrimental consequences of sleep deprivation and shed light on the importance of prioritizing quality sleep for optimal performance and overall well-being.

Sleep is not just a mere act of resting; it is a fundamental physiological need that plays a vital role in maintaining our physical and mental health. When we consistently fail to get enough sleep, whether due to work demands, personal commitments, or lifestyle choices, we expose ourselves to a wide range of negative consequences.

One of the most immediate impacts of sleep deprivation is impaired cognitive function. Lack of sleep affects our ability to concentrate, make decisions, and retain information. It hampers our creativity, problem-solving skills, and overall productivity. We become more prone to errors, accidents, and poor judgment. Moreover, chronic sleep deprivation has been linked to an increased risk of developing neurodegenerative diseases such as Alzheimer's and Parkinson's.

Sleep deprivation also takes a toll on our emotional well-being. It disrupts the delicate balance of hormones responsible for regulating our mood, resulting in increased irritability, mood swings, and heightened stress levels. Prolonged sleep deprivation can contribute to the development of anxiety and depression, making it crucial to address sleep issues as part of mental health management.

Furthermore, sleep deprivation compromises our immune system, leaving us more susceptible to infections and diseases. It raises the risk of developing chronic conditions such as obesity, diabetes, and cardiovascular diseases. Lack of sleep also affects our appetite-regulating hormones, leading to weight gain and an increased craving for unhealthy foods.

To harness the power of sleep and unlock its benefits, it is essential to prioritize adequate and restorative sleep. By adopting healthy sleep habits, such as maintaining a consistent sleep schedule, creating a sleep-friendly environment, and practicing relaxation techniques, we can optimize our sleep quality and duration.

In conclusion, sleep deprivation has far-reaching consequences that impact our cognitive abilities, emotional well-being, and physical health. Recognizing the importance of sleep and taking proactive steps to enhance our sleep hygiene is crucial for unlocking the secrets to optimal sleep and performance. By prioritizing sleep, we can improve our overall quality of life and achieve our full potential in all areas of life.

Short-term effects of sleep deprivation

Sleep is often undervalued and overlooked in today's fast-paced society. Many people prioritize work, socializing, and entertainment over getting adequate sleep, leading to a widespread epidemic of sleep deprivation. In this subchapter, we will explore the short-term effects of sleep deprivation and highlight the importance of prioritizing quality sleep for optimal performance.

When we don't get enough sleep, even just for a night or two, the consequences can be immediate and impactful. One of the most noticeable short-term effects of sleep deprivation is impaired cognitive function. Lack of sleep affects our ability to concentrate, make decisions, and process information efficiently. It becomes harder to stay focused and productive, leading to decreased performance at work, school, or any other task that requires mental acuity.

Sleep deprivation also affects our mood and emotional well-being. When we are sleep-deprived, we are more likely to experience irritability, mood swings, and increased levels of stress. This can strain relationships, hinder communication, and make even the simplest tasks feel overwhelming. Additionally, lack of sleep can contribute to feelings of anxiety and depression, further impacting our mental health.

Furthermore, sleep deprivation can have negative effects on our physical health. It weakens the immune system, making us more susceptible to illnesses such as colds and flu. It also increases the risk of accidents and injuries due to impaired coordination and slower reaction times. Moreover, sleep deprivation disrupts the balance of hormones in our body, leading to increased appetite and cravings for unhealthy foods, which can contribute to weight gain and obesity.

To combat the short-term effects of sleep deprivation, it is crucial to prioritize quality sleep. Establishing a consistent sleep schedule, creating a relaxing bedtime routine, and optimizing your sleep environment can greatly improve your sleep quality. Avoiding stimulants like caffeine and electronic devices before bed and engaging in relaxation techniques such as meditation or reading can help promote a restful night's sleep.

In conclusion, sleep deprivation has significant short-term effects on cognitive function, mood, emotional well-being, and physical health. By recognizing the importance of sleep and making it a priority, we can unlock the secrets to optimal sleep and performance. Prioritizing quality sleep will not only improve our short-term functioning but also have long-term benefits for our overall health and well-being.

Long-term effects of chronic sleep deprivation

Sleep is an essential aspect of our daily lives, yet many people underestimate its power and the detrimental effects of not getting enough of it. Chronic sleep deprivation, which refers to consistently not getting enough sleep over an extended period, can have severe long-term consequences on our health, performance, and overall well-being.

One of the most noticeable effects of chronic sleep deprivation is its impact on cognitive function. Lack of sleep impairs our ability to concentrate, focus, and make decisions. It affects our memory, making it difficult to retain and recall information. This can hinder our learning abilities and academic or professional performance. Additionally, chronic sleep deprivation has been linked to an increased risk of developing mood disorders such as depression and anxiety. It can also exacerbate existing mental health conditions, making them more challenging to manage.

The physical health implications of chronic sleep deprivation are equally concerning. Sleep deprivation weakens the immune system, making individuals more susceptible to infections and illnesses. It has also been linked to an increased risk of developing chronic conditions such as obesity, diabetes, and cardiovascular diseases. Furthermore, sleep deprivation disrupts the hormonal balance in our bodies, leading to increased levels of stress hormones like cortisol. This can contribute to weight gain, high blood pressure, and an increased risk of developing metabolic disorders.

In addition to the cognitive and physical effects, chronic sleep deprivation can also impact our performance and safety. Lack of sleep impairs judgment, reaction time, and coordination, increasing the likelihood of accidents and errors. This is particularly dangerous in professions that require high levels of alertness, such as pilots, doctors, and truck drivers. Chronic sleep deprivation can also negatively affect relationships, as it can lead to irritability, mood swings, and decreased empathy and understanding.

To mitigate the long-term effects of chronic sleep deprivation, it is crucial to prioritize and optimize our sleep routine. Establishing a regular sleep schedule, creating a sleep-friendly environment, and practicing relaxation techniques before bed can greatly improve the quality and duration of our sleep. Additionally, adopting healthy lifestyle habits such as regular exercise, a balanced diet, and stress management techniques can promote better sleep.

In conclusion, chronic sleep deprivation can have significant long-term consequences on our physical and mental health, cognitive abilities, performance, and overall well-being. Recognizing the importance of sleep and prioritizing its quality and quantity is essential for optimal sleep and performance. By adopting healthy sleep habits, we can unlock the secrets to optimal sleep and achieve our full potential in all areas of life.

Impact on cognitive function and performance

Getting enough quality sleep is crucial for maintaining optimal cognitive function and performance in our daily lives. Sleep deprivation can have a profound impact on our mental abilities, affecting our memory, attention, decision-making skills, and overall cognitive performance.

Numerous studies have shown that a lack of sleep can impair our ability to concentrate and retain information. When we are sleep-deprived, our brain's ability to process and consolidate new information is significantly compromised. This can have a detrimental effect on our learning capabilities and make it difficult to perform well in academic or professional settings.

In addition to memory and learning, sleep plays a critical role in our attention span and focus. When we don't get enough sleep, our ability to concentrate on tasks diminishes, leading to decreased productivity and performance. Whether you're a student studying for an exam or a professional working on an important project, insufficient sleep can hinder your ability to stay focused and perform at your best.

Sleep deprivation also impairs our decision-making abilities. When we are tired, our judgment becomes clouded, making it harder to make rational choices. This can affect various aspects of our lives, such as financial decisions, problem-solving, and even social interactions. Lack of sleep can lead to impulsive behavior and poor decision-making, potentially impacting our personal and professional relationships.

Furthermore, sleep deprivation has been linked to an increased risk of accidents and errors. Fatigue-related accidents are prevalent across various industries, including healthcare, transportation, and manufacturing. The diminished cognitive function resulting from lack of sleep can lead to mistakes that can have severe consequences for both individuals and organizations.

On the other hand, prioritizing and optimizing sleep can have tremendous benefits for cognitive function and performance. When we consistently get enough quality sleep, our memory and learning abilities are enhanced. Our brain's ability to process information, consolidate memories, and make connections is optimized during sleep, leading to improved cognitive performance.

Adequate sleep also boosts our attention span and focus, allowing us to stay engaged and productive throughout the day. With enhanced concentration, our ability to perform complex tasks, solve problems, and make better decisions is greatly improved.

In conclusion, sleep has a profound impact on our cognitive function and performance. By understanding the importance of sleep and making it a priority in our lives, we can unlock the secrets to optimal sleep and achieve peak cognitive performance. Whether you are a student, professional, or anyone seeking to enhance their mental abilities, harnessing the power of sleep is essential for success in all aspects of life.

The Sleep-Performance Connection

In today's fast-paced world, where productivity and performance are highly valued, we often sacrifice sleep in the pursuit of success. However, what if I told you that getting optimal sleep is actually the key to unlocking your true potential and enhancing your performance in all areas of life? This subchapter will delve into the fascinating topic of the sleep-performance connection and shed light on why sleep is a powerful tool for achieving success.

When we think of enhancing performance, we often resort to strategies like time management, setting goals, or working harder. While these are all important, we often overlook the most fundamental factor that can significantly impact our performance – sleep. Sleep is not just a time for rest and recovery; it is a critical process that directly affects our cognitive abilities, memory, decision-making skills, and overall brain function.

Numerous studies have established a strong link between sleep and performance. Lack of sleep has been shown to impair attention, concentration, creativity, problem-solving skills, and even physical performance. On the other hand, getting adequate, high-quality sleep has been proven to sharpen cognitive abilities, enhance learning and memory retention, boost creativity, and improve overall mood and well-being.

In this subchapter, we will explore the science behind the sleep-performance connection. We will delve into the different stages of sleep, discussing how each stage contributes to our cognitive and physical abilities. We will also uncover the impact of sleep deprivation on our performance and discuss the long-term consequences of chronic sleep deficiency.

Moreover, we will provide practical tips and strategies for optimizing sleep to unlock your full potential. From creating a sleep-friendly environment and establishing a consistent sleep routine to incorporating relaxation techniques and managing stress, we will equip you with the tools to enhance both the quantity and quality of your sleep.

Remember, sleep is not a luxury; it is a necessity. By prioritizing sleep, you are investing in your performance and well-being. Whether you are a student striving for academic success, an athlete aiming for peak performance, or a professional looking to excel in your career, understanding and harnessing the power of sleep is crucial.

So, join us on this enlightening journey as we explore the sleep-performance connection and unlock the secrets to optimal sleep and performance. Get ready to awaken your true potential and achieve new heights of success through the power of sleep.

How sleep affects productivity and efficiency

In today's fast-paced world, sleep is often overlooked as a luxury rather than recognized for its essential role in our overall well-being. However, science has consistently shown that sleep is a crucial component of optimal health, productivity, and efficiency. In this subchapter, we will explore the powerful connection between sleep and our ability to perform at our best.

One of the most significant ways sleep affects productivity is through its impact on cognitive function. When we are sleep-deprived, our brain's ability to concentrate, problem-solve, and make decisions is greatly impaired. Studies have shown that even a night of poor sleep can result in decreased attention span, reduced creativity, and slower reaction times. On the other hand, getting sufficient sleep has been linked to enhanced memory, improved focus, and heightened mental clarity – all of which are essential for productivity and efficiency.

Furthermore, sleep plays a crucial role in regulating our emotions and mood. Lack of sleep has been strongly associated with increased irritability, mood swings, and a higher likelihood of experiencing stress and anxiety. This emotional instability can significantly impact our productivity, as it interferes with our ability to stay calm, focused, and motivated. On the contrary, when we prioritize quality sleep, we are more likely to be in a positive state of mind, enabling us to approach tasks with enthusiasm and tackle challenges effectively.

Another important aspect to consider is the physical impact of sleep on productivity. When we are sleep-deprived, our bodies experience increased fatigue, decreased energy levels, and reduced physical performance. This can lead to decreased efficiency in completing physical tasks and a higher risk of making mistakes. On the other hand, when we allow our bodies to rest and recover through adequate sleep, we experience improved physical stamina, increased energy, and enhanced coordination – all factors that contribute to higher productivity levels.

It is also worth mentioning the long-term effects of chronic sleep deprivation. Consistently failing to prioritize sleep can lead to serious health consequences such as weight gain, weakened immune system, and an increased risk of developing chronic conditions like diabetes and heart disease. These health issues can further hinder productivity and efficiency by causing frequent absences, decreased cognitive function, and decreased overall well-being.

In conclusion, sleep is not just a luxury but a powerful tool that can significantly impact our productivity and efficiency. By understanding and valuing the importance of sleep, we can unlock the secrets to optimal performance in all areas of our lives. Prioritizing quality sleep, ensuring a consistent sleep schedule, creating a sleep-friendly environment, and adopting healthy sleep habits can all contribute to maximizing our productivity and efficiency, allowing us to achieve our goals and live our best lives.

Enhancing athletic performance through sleep

Sleep is a crucial aspect of our overall health and well-being, and it plays a significant role in athletic performance. In the fast-paced world we live in today, sleep is often undervalued and neglected. However, understanding the power of sleep and incorporating it into our routine can be a game-changer for athletes and anyone seeking optimal performance.

Athletes are constantly pushing their bodies to the limit, and sleep is where the magic happens. During sleep, our bodies undergo essential processes that repair and restore muscles, regulate hormones, and consolidate memories, all of which contribute to enhancing athletic performance.

One of the key benefits of sleep for athletes is muscle recovery. Intense physical activity causes microscopic damage to muscle fibers, and it is during sleep that these fibers repair themselves, becoming stronger and more resilient. Quality sleep also promotes the release of growth hormones, which aid in muscle repair and growth.

Sleep is also closely linked to cognitive function, which is essential for optimal performance in sports. During sleep, the brain processes and consolidates information, enhancing memory and decision-making skills. This is particularly crucial for athletes who need to analyze complex game situations and react quickly.

Furthermore, sleep deprivation negatively impacts athletic performance in several ways. Lack of sleep can lead to decreased reaction time, impaired judgment, and reduced focus and concentration. It can also increase the risk of injuries, as fatigue compromises coordination and balance. Sleep deprivation also disrupts the body's ability to regulate insulin, leading to decreased energy levels and impaired recovery.

To enhance athletic performance through sleep, it is important to prioritize sleep hygiene. This includes maintaining a consistent sleep schedule, creating a sleep-friendly environment, and practicing relaxation techniques before bed. Additionally, avoiding stimulating activities, such as electronic devices, before sleep can improve sleep quality.

In conclusion, sleep plays a crucial role in enhancing athletic performance. By recognizing the power of sleep and prioritizing it in our daily routine, athletes and individuals seeking optimal performance can reap the benefits of improved muscle recovery, cognitive function, and overall well-being. So, whether you are an athlete or simply someone striving for peak performance, don't underestimate the power of a good night's sleep.

Sleep's impact on creativity and problem-solving abilities

In today's fast-paced and demanding world, sleep has often taken a backseat in our quest for success and productivity. We tend to overlook the fact that sleep plays a crucial role in not only our physical well-being but also our cognitive abilities. In this subchapter, we will delve into the fascinating connection between sleep and creativity, as well as problem-solving abilities.

It is no secret that a good night's sleep can leave us feeling refreshed and rejuvenated, but did you know that it also has a direct impact on our creativity? When we sleep, our brain goes through different stages, including deep sleep and rapid eye movement (REM) sleep. These stages are essential for consolidating memories and organizing information, which are vital for creative thinking.

During REM sleep, our brain is highly active, and it is during this stage that we often experience vivid dreams. Research has shown that REM sleep is linked to creative problem-solving and the formation of new ideas. It is during this stage that our brain makes connections between seemingly unrelated concepts, leading to unique and innovative solutions.

Additionally, a well-rested mind is more open to diverse perspectives and out-of-the-box thinking. When we are sleep-deprived, our cognitive processes become hindered, leading to a narrowed focus and reduced ability to think creatively. On the other hand, a good night's sleep enhances our ability to think laterally, make connections between seemingly disparate ideas, and come up with novel solutions to complex problems.

Furthermore, sleep has a significant impact on our problem-solving abilities. Research has consistently shown that a well-rested mind is better equipped to analyze and solve problems efficiently. Sleep deprivation impairs our cognitive functions, making it harder to concentrate, make decisions, and think critically. In contrast, a good night's sleep enhances our ability to think clearly, improve attention, and retain information, all of which are crucial for effective problem-solving.

To harness the power of sleep for optimal creativity and problem-solving abilities, it is important to prioritize sleep in our daily routine. Creating a sleep-friendly environment, maintaining a consistent sleep schedule, and practicing relaxation techniques can all contribute to better sleep quality.

In conclusion, sleep is not just a necessary bodily function but a key ingredient for unlocking our creative potential and problem-solving abilities. By understanding and prioritizing the power of sleep, we can optimize our cognitive functions, enhance creativity, and improve our overall performance in both personal and professional pursuits.

Chapter 2: Unlocking the Secrets to Quality Sleep

Creating an Optimal Sleep Environment

Creating an optimal sleep environment is crucial for achieving restful and rejuvenating sleep. In this subchapter, we will explore the key elements that contribute to a conducive sleep environment, allowing you to unlock the secrets to optimal sleep and performance. Whether you are a busy professional, a student, or someone seeking to improve their overall well-being, understanding the power of sleep and implementing these strategies can transform your life.

One of the first steps towards creating an optimal sleep environment is ensuring that your bedroom is a peaceful and relaxing sanctuary. Remove any distractions that may interfere with your sleep, such as electronics, bright lights, or loud noises. Consider investing in blackout curtains or an eye mask to block out any unwanted light, as well as earplugs or a white noise machine to drown out any disruptive sounds.

Temperature plays a significant role in sleep quality. Keep your bedroom cool, ideally between 60-67 degrees Fahrenheit, as a cooler environment promotes better sleep. Additionally, choose bedding and sleepwear that are comfortable and suitable for the climate, allowing your body to maintain an optimal temperature throughout the night.

Your mattress and pillows are essential components of a conducive sleep environment. Invest in a high-quality mattress that provides the right level of support for your body, ensuring proper spinal alignment. Similarly, select pillows that adequately support your neck and head, allowing for comfortable and restful sleep.

Creating a bedtime routine is another effective way to optimize your sleep environment. Establish a consistent sleep schedule, going to bed and waking up at the same time each day. This helps regulate your body's internal clock and promotes better sleep quality. Incorporate relaxation techniques into your routine, such as reading a book, practicing deep breathing exercises, or taking a warm bath, to signal to your body that it's time to wind down and prepare for sleep.

Lastly, ensure that your sleep environment is clean and clutter-free. A tidy bedroom promotes a sense of calm and relaxation, allowing you to unwind more easily. Keep technology out of the bedroom, as the blue light emitted from screens can disrupt your circadian rhythm and interfere with sleep quality.

By implementing these strategies and creating an optimal sleep environment, you harness the power of sleep to enhance your overall well-being and performance. Whether you're seeking to improve your productivity, mental clarity, or physical health, prioritizing sleep and creating the right conditions for restful sleep will undoubtedly unlock your true potential.

Designing a comfortable and conducive bedroom

A good night's sleep is crucial for our overall well-being and performance. Creating a bedroom that is comfortable and conducive to sleep can make a significant difference in the quality of rest we get each night. In this subchapter, we will explore various elements and tips to help you design the perfect sleep sanctuary.

First and foremost, let's talk about the importance of a comfortable mattress and pillows. Investing in a high-quality, supportive mattress that suits your body type and sleeping position can do wonders for your sleep. Similarly, choosing pillows that provide adequate neck support will help prevent any discomfort during the night.

Consider the overall design and layout of your bedroom. Opt for soothing colors and soft lighting to create a relaxing atmosphere. Avoid clutter and keep the room neat and organized, as a messy environment can cause unnecessary stress and restlessness. Remember, your bedroom should be a sanctuary for sleep, so keep distractions like electronics, work materials, and exercise equipment to a minimum.

Temperature and ventilation play crucial roles in promoting a restful sleep. Keep your bedroom cool, ideally between 60-67 degrees Fahrenheit, to facilitate the body's natural temperature drop during sleep. Additionally, proper ventilation ensures a constant supply of fresh air, creating a pleasant sleeping environment.

Noise can disrupt sleep and prevent you from reaching deep, restorative stages. Consider using earplugs or white noise machines to block out any disturbances. If you live in a noisy area, consider installing soundproof windows or using heavy curtains to dampen outside sounds.

Lastly, pay attention to the textiles in your bedroom. Choose high-quality, breathable bedding that feels soft and comfortable against your skin. Natural fabrics like cotton and linen are excellent choices as they allow for better air circulation and moisture-wicking properties.

By implementing these tips, you can transform your bedroom into a haven for optimal sleep. Remember, a restful night sets the stage for a productive day ahead. Take the time to create a sleep-friendly environment, and you'll reap the benefits of improved sleep quality and overall well-being.

Whether you are a working professional, a student, or simply someone who wants to unlock the power of sleep, designing a comfortable and conducive bedroom is a vital step towards achieving optimal sleep and performance.

The ideal room temperature and lighting for sleep

The ideal room temperature and lighting for sleep are crucial factors that can significantly impact the quality of our sleep. Achieving a comfortable room temperature and creating a sleep-friendly lighting environment are essential steps towards unlocking the power of sleep.

When it comes to the ideal room temperature for sleep, research suggests that a slightly cooler environment tends to promote better sleep. The recommended temperature range falls between 60 to 67 degrees Fahrenheit (15 to 19 degrees Celsius). This temperature range helps to signal the body that it's time for rest, as our core body temperature naturally drops during sleep. By maintaining a cooler room temperature, we create an optimal sleep environment that facilitates falling asleep faster and staying asleep throughout the night.

In addition to temperature, lighting also plays a crucial role in promoting restful sleep. Exposure to bright lights in the evenings, especially blue light emitted by electronic devices, can disrupt our natural sleep-wake cycle. Blue light suppresses the production of melatonin, the hormone responsible for regulating sleep. To create a sleep-friendly lighting environment, it is recommended to dim the lights in the evening and avoid using electronic devices at least an hour before bed. Consider using warm, soft lighting or even candlelight to create a calming atmosphere that signals your body it's time to wind down.

By prioritizing the ideal room temperature and lighting for sleep, we enhance our ability to fall asleep faster, stay asleep longer, and experience more restorative sleep. Optimizing these factors contributes to our overall well-being and unlocks the full potential of our sleep.

Implementing these strategies can positively impact not only our physical health but also our cognitive function, mood, and performance during the day. Quality sleep is a powerful tool that allows us to optimize our productivity, creativity, and decision-making abilities. It is an essential pillar of the Power of Sleep.

In conclusion, understanding and implementing the ideal room temperature and lighting for sleep can have a profound impact on our sleep quality and overall performance. By creating a comfortable sleep environment, we can unlock the secrets to optimal sleep and harness the power of sleep for a healthier, happier, and more productive life.

The impact of noise and technology on sleep quality

In today's fast-paced, technology-driven world, many of us struggle to get a good night's sleep. We often find ourselves tossing and turning, unable to fall asleep or stay asleep throughout the night. While there are many factors that can affect sleep quality, two of the most significant culprits are noise and technology.

Noise pollution has become an increasingly prevalent issue in our modern society. Whether it's the sound of traffic outside our window, the blaring sirens of emergency vehicles, or even the hum of electronics in our own homes, noise can have a profound impact on our ability to sleep. Studies have shown that exposure to excessive noise can disrupt sleep patterns, leading to decreased sleep quality and increased daytime sleepiness. This can have a cascading effect on our overall health and well-being, leading to decreased productivity, impaired cognitive function, and even an increased risk of chronic health conditions.

Similarly, the invasion of technology into our bedrooms has become a pervasive problem. Many of us are guilty of using our smartphones, tablets, or laptops right before bed, unaware of the detrimental effects this can have on our sleep. The blue light emitted by these devices can interfere with the production of melatonin, the hormone that regulates our sleep-wake cycle. This can disrupt our natural circadian rhythm, making it harder for us to fall asleep and stay asleep throughout the night. Additionally, the constant notifications and distractions from technology can heighten our stress levels and keep our minds racing, further hindering our ability to achieve restful sleep.

So, what can we do to combat the negative impact of noise and technology on our sleep quality? One simple solution is to create a sleep-friendly environment. This includes investing in earplugs or a white noise machine to block out external noises, as well as removing electronic devices from the bedroom or using apps that filter out blue light. Establishing a consistent bedtime routine that incorporates relaxation techniques, such as reading a book or taking a warm bath, can also help signal to our bodies that it's time to wind down and prepare for sleep.

In conclusion, the impact of noise and technology on sleep quality cannot be understated. By understanding the detrimental effects of noise pollution and technology on our sleep, and implementing strategies to mitigate these factors, we can improve our overall sleep quality and unlock the secrets to optimal sleep and performance. Remember, the power of sleep should never be underestimated, and it's up to us to prioritize and protect our sleep to lead healthier, more productive lives.

Developing a Consistent Sleep Routine

In today's fast-paced world, getting a good night's sleep may seem like a luxury. With endless to-do lists, work pressures, and the constant stimulation of technology, sleep often takes a backseat. However, understanding the power of sleep and prioritizing it in our lives can have a profound impact on our overall well-being and performance. In this subchapter, we will explore the importance of developing a consistent sleep routine and how it can unlock the secrets to optimal sleep and performance.

Consistency is key when it comes to sleep. Our bodies thrive on routine, and establishing a consistent sleep schedule helps align our internal clock, known as the circadian rhythm. By going to bed and waking up at the same time every day, even on weekends, we train our bodies to recognize when it's time to sleep and when it's time to wake up. This regularity enhances the quality and duration of our sleep, leading to improved cognitive function, increased energy levels, and better overall health.

Creating a sleep routine involves more than just setting a bedtime. It's about creating a relaxing and conducive environment for sleep. Dimming the lights, avoiding stimulating activities before bed, and establishing a calming bedtime routine, such as reading or meditating, can signal our brain that it's time to unwind and prepare for sleep. Additionally, ensuring that our sleep environment is comfortable, cool, and free from distractions like electronic devices can further enhance our sleep quality.

Understanding the power of sleep also means recognizing the impact of our daytime habits on our sleep. Regular exercise, exposure to natural light, and a balanced diet can all contribute to better sleep.

Engaging in physical activity during the day helps regulate our sleep-wake cycle, while exposure to natural light helps synchronize our circadian rhythm. Furthermore, adopting a healthy diet rich in sleep-promoting nutrients, such as magnesium and tryptophan, can improve sleep quality.

In conclusion, developing a consistent sleep routine is vital for harnessing the power of sleep. By aligning our sleep schedule, creating a relaxing sleep environment, and adopting healthy daytime habits, we can unlock the secrets to optimal sleep and performance. Remember, sleep is not a luxury but a necessity for our overall well-being. So, let's prioritize sleep, and watch as it transforms our lives for the better.

Establishing a regular sleep-wake schedule

In our fast-paced and demanding world, it's easy to overlook the importance of a regular sleep-wake schedule. However, understanding the power of sleep and its impact on our overall performance is crucial for anyone seeking optimal health and success. In this subchapter, we will explore the benefits of establishing a regular sleep-wake schedule and provide practical tips to help you achieve a more consistent and restorative sleep routine.

Sleep is a fundamental biological need that affects every aspect of our lives, from our physical health to our cognitive abilities. By maintaining a regular sleep-wake schedule, you can align your body's natural rhythms and optimize the quality and quantity of your sleep. Consistency in your sleep schedule helps regulate your internal body clock, known as the circadian rhythm, which governs various physiological processes.

One of the key benefits of a regular sleep-wake schedule is improved sleep quality. When you go to bed and wake up at the same time every day, your body becomes accustomed to a set routine, making it easier to fall asleep and wake up naturally. This leads to more restful and rejuvenating sleep, allowing you to wake up feeling refreshed and energized.

Moreover, a regular sleep-wake schedule promotes better overall health. Research has shown that irregular sleep patterns can disrupt hormone production, weaken the immune system, and increase the risk of chronic conditions such as obesity, diabetes, and cardiovascular disease. By prioritizing a consistent sleep routine, you can mitigate these risks and enhance your overall well-being.

Establishing a regular sleep-wake schedule requires discipline and a mindful approach. Start by setting a consistent bedtime and wake-up time, even on weekends. Create a relaxing pre-sleep routine that helps signal your body that it's time to wind down. This may include activities such as reading a book, taking a warm bath, or practicing relaxation techniques.

Additionally, it's important to create an optimal sleep environment. Keep your bedroom cool, dark, and quiet, and invest in a comfortable mattress and pillows that support your body's needs. Limit exposure to electronic devices before bedtime, as the blue light emitted by screens can disrupt your natural sleep-wake cycle.

In conclusion, establishing a regular sleep-wake schedule is essential for harnessing the power of sleep and optimizing your performance in all areas of life. By prioritizing consistent sleep patterns, you can improve sleep quality, enhance overall health, and unlock your full potential. So, set those consistent bedtimes and wake-up times, create a relaxing sleep routine, and transform your sleep habits to unlock the secrets to optimal sleep and performance.

The importance of winding down before bed

In our fast-paced, always-on society, it's becoming increasingly difficult to disconnect from the demands of the day and give our bodies and minds the rest they truly need. We often find ourselves glued to our screens, scrolling through social media, or catching up on work until the late hours of the night. However, the truth is, this lack of winding down before bedtime can have detrimental effects on our sleep quality and overall well-being.

Sleep is a vital component of our lives, and it is during this time that our bodies repair and restore themselves. Without proper sleep, our cognitive functions are impaired, our immune system weakened, and we become more susceptible to a range of health issues. That's why it's crucial to prioritize winding down before bed and create a relaxing routine that will prepare our bodies and minds for a restful night's sleep.

One of the key benefits of winding down before bed is that it signals to your body that it's time to shift into sleep mode. By engaging in calming activities such as reading a book, taking a warm bath, or practicing relaxation techniques like deep breathing or meditation, you can help lower your heart rate, reduce stress levels, and promote a sense of tranquility. These activities allow your body to release tension and transition into a state of relaxation, making it easier to fall asleep and stay asleep throughout the night.

Winding down before bed also helps to improve the quality of your sleep. When you give yourself time to unwind, you're more likely to experience deeper, more restorative sleep cycles. This is because your body has had the opportunity to release any built-up tension or stress, allowing for a more peaceful and rejuvenating slumber. On the other hand, if you go to bed immediately after engaging in stimulating activities or being exposed to bright lights from screens, your sleep may be disrupted, leading to a restless night and feeling groggy the next day.

Furthermore, winding down before bed can have a positive impact on your overall well-being. It provides an opportunity for self-care and reflection, allowing you to prioritize your mental and emotional health. This uninterrupted time allows you to disconnect from the outside world, focus on yourself, and cultivate a sense of calm and inner peace. By adopting a consistent winding-down routine, you can create a sanctuary for yourself before bed, where you can unwind, recharge, and prepare for a better tomorrow.

In conclusion, the importance of winding down before bed cannot be overstated. It is a crucial component of optimal sleep and performance. By prioritizing a relaxing routine, you can signal to your body that it's time to rest, improve the quality of your sleep, and enhance your overall well-being. So, tonight, make a commitment to yourself and take the necessary steps to wind down before bed. Your body and mind will thank you for it.

Implementing relaxation techniques to promote better sleep

In today's fast-paced world, many of us struggle with getting a good night's sleep. The constant demands of work, family, and social obligations can leave us feeling stressed, anxious, and unable to unwind when it's time to sleep. However, implementing relaxation techniques can be a game-changer when it comes to achieving better sleep and improving overall well-being.

One powerful tool in combating sleep issues is the practice of relaxation techniques. These techniques can help calm the mind and body, reduce stress levels, and prepare us for a restful night's sleep. By incorporating these practices into our daily routine, we can create an environment conducive to better sleep and wake up feeling refreshed and energized.

One effective relaxation technique is deep breathing exercises. By focusing on our breath and taking slow, deep breaths, we activate the body's relaxation response. This helps to slow down the heart rate, relax the muscles, and quiet the mind. Deep breathing exercises can be done anywhere, anytime, and are a simple yet powerful way to promote better sleep.

Another technique is progressive muscle relaxation. This involves systematically tensing and then relaxing each muscle group in the body, starting from the toes and working our way up to the head. By consciously releasing tension in the muscles, we can release tension in the mind as well, leading to a more peaceful and restful sleep.

Meditation is another powerful relaxation technique that can promote better sleep. By practicing mindfulness meditation, we can train our minds to focus on the present moment and let go of racing thoughts and worries that can keep us awake at night. Regular meditation practice has been shown to improve sleep quality and duration.

In addition to these techniques, incorporating a bedtime routine can also help signal to the body that it's time to wind down and prepare for sleep. This can include activities such as reading a book, taking a warm bath, or listening to calming music. Creating a relaxing environment in the bedroom, such as keeping it cool, dark, and free from distractions, can also contribute to better sleep.

Implementing relaxation techniques to promote better sleep is a powerful way to tap into the power of sleep. By taking the time to relax and unwind before bed, we can improve the quality of our sleep, enhance our overall well-being, and unlock the secrets to optimal sleep and performance. So, why not give these techniques a try and experience the transformative effects of better sleep for yourself?

Optimizing Sleep through Nutrition and Exercise

In today's fast-paced world, sleep has often taken a backseat to our busy lives. However, research has shown that the power of sleep cannot be underestimated when it comes to achieving optimal performance in life. In this subchapter, we will explore the ways in which nutrition and exercise can play a crucial role in optimizing your sleep.

Nutrition plays a vital role in our overall health, and it directly affects our sleep patterns. Certain foods can help promote a restful night's sleep, while others can disrupt it. For instance, consuming foods rich in tryptophan, such as turkey, nuts, and seeds, can increase the production of serotonin, a hormone that helps regulate sleep. Including these foods in your evening meals can promote better sleep quality.

Similarly, avoiding certain foods and beverages can also contribute to a good night's sleep. Foods high in sugar, caffeine, and processed ingredients can interfere with our sleep patterns. Consuming these substances close to bedtime can lead to restlessness and difficulty falling asleep. Instead, opt for a light snack that contains complex carbohydrates and protein, such as a small bowl of oatmeal or a handful of almonds.

Exercise is another essential component when it comes to optimizing sleep. Regular physical activity helps to regulate the circadian rhythm, our body's internal clock responsible for maintaining our sleep-wake cycle. Engaging in moderate-intensity exercise, such as brisk walking or cycling, for at least 30 minutes a day can significantly improve sleep quality. However, it is important to avoid exercising too close to bedtime, as the increased heart rate and adrenaline release can make it difficult to fall asleep.

In addition to nutrition and exercise, there are other lifestyle factors that can contribute to better sleep. Establishing a consistent sleep routine, creating a sleep-friendly environment, and managing stress levels are all crucial elements in maximizing sleep quality.

In conclusion, optimizing sleep through nutrition and exercise is a powerful tool for achieving optimal performance in life. By nourishing our bodies with sleep-promoting foods and engaging in regular physical activity, we can enhance the quality and duration of our sleep. So, let's prioritize our sleep and unlock the secrets to optimal sleep and performance.

Foods that promote better sleep

In today's fast-paced world, getting quality sleep has become more important than ever. Lack of sleep can lead to a host of health issues and negatively impact our performance during the day. However, did you know that the food we consume can play a significant role in promoting better sleep? By incorporating certain foods into our diet, we can optimize our sleep patterns and achieve a more restful night. In this subchapter, we will explore the power of sleep-promoting foods and how they can benefit anyone striving for optimal sleep and performance.

One of the key nutrients that can enhance sleep quality is tryptophan. Tryptophan is an amino acid that helps the body produce serotonin and melatonin, two hormones crucial for regulating sleep. Foods rich in tryptophan include turkey, chicken, tofu, nuts, and seeds. Consuming these foods can help increase the production of sleep-inducing hormones and promote a more restful sleep.

Another group of foods that can aid in better sleep are those high in magnesium. Magnesium is a mineral that helps relax the muscles and calm the nervous system. Incorporating magnesium-rich foods like leafy greens, legumes, whole grains, and bananas into your diet can contribute to a more relaxed state before bedtime, making it easier to fall asleep and stay asleep throughout the night.

Additionally, foods rich in calcium can also promote better sleep. Calcium helps the brain use tryptophan to produce melatonin, the hormone responsible for regulating sleep. Dairy products, such as milk and yogurt, are excellent sources of calcium and can be consumed as part of a bedtime routine to encourage deeper and more restorative sleep.

It is worth mentioning that while certain foods can promote better sleep, it is equally important to avoid foods that can disrupt sleep. Stimulants like caffeine and alcohol can interfere with the quality and quantity of sleep, so it is advisable to limit their consumption, particularly in the hours leading up to bedtime.

In conclusion, the power of sleep-promoting foods cannot be underestimated. By incorporating tryptophan-rich foods, magnesium-rich foods, and calcium-rich foods into our diet, we can optimize our sleep patterns and achieve a more restful night's sleep. Furthermore, being mindful of avoiding sleep-disrupting foods can further enhance the quality of our sleep. With the right nutrition, we can unlock the secrets to optimal sleep and performance, improving our overall health and well-being.

The role of exercise in improving sleep quality

Exercise is a powerful tool that can significantly enhance our sleep quality and overall well-being. In this subchapter, we will explore the profound impact of exercise on our sleep patterns and delve into the science behind this correlation. Whether you are an athlete, a busy professional, or simply someone seeking better sleep, understanding the role of exercise in improving sleep quality is crucial.

Numerous studies have shown a direct link between regular exercise and improved sleep. Engaging in physical activity helps regulate our internal body clock, known as the circadian rhythm, which controls our sleep-wake cycle. Regular exercise promotes a more consistent sleep schedule, making it easier to fall asleep and wake up at the desired times.

Exercise also helps reduce stress and anxiety, which are common factors that disrupt sleep. Physical activity releases endorphins, known as the "feel-good" hormones, which elevate our mood and promote relaxation. By reducing stress levels, exercise allows us to unwind and prepare our bodies for a restful night's sleep.

Furthermore, engaging in moderate to vigorous exercise increases the time spent in deep sleep, also known as slow-wave sleep. This stage of sleep is crucial for our physical and mental restoration, as it promotes tissue repair, muscle growth, and memory consolidation. By incorporating exercise into our routine, we can enhance the quality of our slow-wave sleep, leading to greater physical recovery and cognitive performance.

It is important to note that timing plays a crucial role in the effectiveness of exercise on sleep quality. Vigorous exercise close to bedtime can actually hinder sleep as it raises our core body temperature and stimulates the release of adrenaline. Therefore, it is recommended to complete your workout at least a few hours before bedtime to allow your body temperature to return to normal.

In conclusion, exercise is a powerful tool that can significantly improve sleep quality. By regulating our internal body clock, reducing stress levels, and promoting deep sleep, exercise offers a multitude of benefits for our sleep-wake cycle. Whether you are an athlete seeking optimal performance or someone simply looking for better sleep, incorporating regular exercise into your routine can unlock the secrets to optimal sleep and performance.

Timing meals and workouts for optimal sleep benefits

In our fast-paced society, it's easy to neglect the importance of sleep and prioritize other aspects of our lives. However, understanding the power of sleep and how it directly affects our performance is crucial for overall well-being. In this subchapter, we will explore the significance of timing meals and workouts to achieve optimal sleep benefits.

When it comes to sleep, the timing of our meals can play a significant role. Eating heavy meals right before bed can lead to discomfort and indigestion, making it difficult to fall asleep. It's best to have your dinner at least two to three hours before bedtime, allowing your body enough time to digest the food properly. By giving your body a chance to digest, you can avoid disruptions in your sleep, ensuring a more restful night.

On the other hand, going to bed hungry can also disrupt your sleep. If you find yourself craving a late-night snack, opt for a light, sleep-friendly option such as a small piece of fruit or a handful of nuts. These choices provide essential nutrients without causing discomfort or interfering with your sleep patterns.

In addition to meal timing, coordinating your workouts with your sleep schedule can also enhance your sleep quality. Engaging in strenuous exercise too close to bedtime can increase your heart rate and body temperature, making it harder to fall asleep. It's recommended to finish your workout at least three hours before bedtime, giving your body ample time to cool down and relax.

Alternatively, incorporating gentle exercise such as yoga or stretching in the evening can promote relaxation and aid in better sleep. These activities help release tension from your muscles and calm your mind, preparing you for a restorative night's sleep.

By understanding the importance of timing meals and workouts for optimal sleep benefits, you can unlock the power of sleep and elevate your overall performance. Prioritizing a balanced diet, avoiding heavy meals before bed, and scheduling workouts strategically can significantly improve your sleep quality and ensure you wake up feeling refreshed and energized.

Remember, sleep is not merely a luxury; it is a vital component of your overall well-being. By implementing these simple strategies, you can harness the power of sleep to unlock your true potential in every aspect of your life.

Chapter 3: Overcoming Common Sleep Challenges

Managing Insomnia and Sleep Disorders

Are you tired of constantly tossing and turning at night, unable to achieve a restful night's sleep? Do you find yourself feeling fatigued and sluggish throughout the day, unable to maintain the energy and focus required for optimal performance? If so, you are not alone. Insomnia and sleep disorders affect millions of individuals worldwide, leading to detrimental effects on both physical and mental health. However, with the right strategies and knowledge, you can take control of your sleep and improve your overall well-being.

In this subchapter, we will explore effective techniques for managing insomnia and sleep disorders, allowing you to unlock the secrets to optimal sleep and performance. First and foremost, it is crucial to establish a consistent sleep routine. By going to bed and waking up at the same time every day, you train your body to recognize when it is time to sleep, promoting a more natural and restful slumber.

Additionally, creating a sleep-friendly environment is essential for a good night's rest. Keep your bedroom cool, dark, and quiet, eliminating any distractions that may interfere with your sleep. Investing in a comfortable mattress and pillows that suit your preferences can also significantly improve your sleep quality.

Furthermore, managing stress levels is vital in combating insomnia and sleep disorders. Incorporating relaxation techniques such as deep breathing exercises, meditation, or yoga before bed can help calm the mind and prepare it for sleep. It is also crucial to limit exposure to electronic devices, as the blue light emitted by screens can disrupt your natural sleep-wake cycle.

In some cases, lifestyle changes alone may not be sufficient to overcome sleep issues. If you continue to struggle with insomnia or sleep disorders despite implementing healthy habits, it may be beneficial to seek professional help. Consulting with a sleep specialist or healthcare provider can provide valuable insights into your condition and guide you towards effective treatments or therapies.

Remember, sleep is a powerful tool that can enhance your performance in all areas of life. By managing insomnia and sleep disorders, you can unlock the secrets to optimal sleep and performance, leading to improved physical health, increased focus, enhanced mood, and overall well-being.

In conclusion, managing insomnia and sleep disorders requires a multifaceted approach that encompasses establishing a consistent sleep routine, creating a sleep-friendly environment, managing stress levels, and seeking professional help when needed. By prioritizing and optimizing your sleep, you will unlock the power of sleep and unleash your true potential.

Understanding insomnia and its causes

Insomnia, a common sleep disorder, affects millions of people worldwide, and its impact on our health and well-being cannot be underestimated. In this subchapter, we will delve into the intricacies of insomnia, exploring its causes and shedding light on its effects on our daily lives. By understanding this sleep disorder, we can take proactive steps towards better sleep and overall improved performance.

Insomnia is characterized by the persistent difficulty in falling asleep or staying asleep, even when given ample opportunity to do so. It can manifest in various ways, such as taking longer than 30 minutes to fall asleep, waking up frequently during the night, or waking up too early and being unable to fall back asleep. While occasional sleep disruptions are normal, chronic insomnia can have a significant impact on our physical and mental health.

There are several factors that can contribute to the development of insomnia. One of the primary causes is stress. Our busy modern lives, filled with work pressures, family responsibilities, and financial worries, can create a constant state of mental and emotional tension, making it difficult to unwind and fall asleep. Additionally, poor sleep habits, such as irregular sleep schedules or excessive caffeine consumption, can disrupt our natural sleep-wake cycle, leading to insomnia.

Another common cause of insomnia is underlying medical conditions. Conditions like chronic pain, sleep apnea, restless leg syndrome, and mental health disorders such as anxiety and depression can all interfere with our ability to achieve restful sleep. Understanding these potential underlying causes is crucial in addressing and managing insomnia effectively.

In the book Sleep Smarter: Unlocking the Secrets to Optimal Sleep and Performance, we explore various strategies to combat insomnia and improve the quality of our sleep. From implementing relaxation techniques and creating a sleep-friendly environment to adopting healthy lifestyle habits and seeking professional help when needed, we provide practical advice tailored to the unique needs of each individual.

Remember, sleep is a powerful tool that can enhance our overall well-being and performance. By understanding insomnia and its causes, we can take the necessary steps towards achieving the restorative sleep we deserve. Together, let's unlock the power of sleep and optimize our lives.

Strategies for overcoming insomnia naturally

Getting a good night's sleep is essential for our overall health and well-being. However, many people struggle with insomnia, a sleep disorder that makes it difficult to fall asleep or stay asleep. If you find yourself tossing and turning in bed night after night, it's time to take action and overcome insomnia naturally. Here are some effective strategies to help you achieve restful sleep and unlock the power of sleep.

1. Establish a Consistent Sleep Routine: Set a fixed bedtime and wake-up time, even on weekends. This helps regulate your body's internal clock and trains it to anticipate sleep at the same time every night.

2. Create a Relaxing Bedtime Ritual: Engage in calming activities before bed, such as reading a book, taking a warm bath, or practicing deep breathing exercises. Avoid stimulating activities and electronic devices that emit blue light, as they can disrupt your sleep cycle.

3. Optimize Your Sleep Environment: Make sure your bedroom is comfortable, cool, dark, and quiet. Invest in a supportive mattress and pillows, use blackout curtains or an eye mask, and consider using earplugs or a white noise machine to drown out any disruptive noises.

4. Practice Stress Management: Stress and anxiety often contribute to insomnia. Find healthy ways to manage stress, such as practicing mindfulness meditation, yoga, or engaging in regular physical exercise. These activities can help calm your mind and prepare your body for quality sleep.

5. Limit Caffeine and Alcohol Intake: Both caffeine and alcohol can interfere with your sleep patterns. Avoid consuming these substances close to bedtime, as they can disrupt your sleep quality and lead to wakefulness during the night.

6. Avoid Heavy Meals Before Bed: Eating large, heavy meals before bedtime can cause discomfort and make it harder to fall asleep. Instead, opt for a light, balanced dinner a few hours before bed and avoid eating close to your bedtime.

7. Create a Sleep-Friendly Diet: Certain foods can promote better sleep, such as complex carbohydrates, lean proteins, and foods rich in tryptophan and magnesium. Incorporate sleep-friendly foods like whole grains, leafy greens, nuts, and seeds into your diet.

Remember, overcoming insomnia naturally takes time and patience. It is essential to have realistic expectations and be consistent in implementing these strategies. By prioritizing your sleep and adopting healthy sleep habits, you can unlock the secrets to optimal sleep and performance, improving your overall quality of life.

Seeking professional help for chronic sleep disorders

In today's fast-paced world, sleep disorders have become increasingly common, affecting millions of people worldwide. Whether it's insomnia, sleep apnea, or restless leg syndrome, these chronic sleep disorders can have a significant impact on our overall health and well-being. While there are various self-help techniques and lifestyle changes that can improve sleep quality, sometimes seeking professional help is necessary to effectively manage these disorders.

One of the first steps in seeking professional help for chronic sleep disorders is to consult with a healthcare provider. They can assess your symptoms, medical history, and perform any necessary tests to diagnose the specific sleep disorder you may be experiencing. This initial evaluation is crucial in determining the most appropriate course of treatment.

One common treatment option for sleep disorders is cognitive behavioral therapy for insomnia (CBT-I). This therapy aims to identify and change the negative thoughts and behaviors that contribute to poor sleep. It may involve techniques such as sleep restriction, stimulus control, and relaxation training. CBT-I has been shown to be highly effective in improving sleep quality and reducing the reliance on sleep medications.

For more severe sleep disorders like sleep apnea, a sleep study may be recommended. This involves spending a night at a sleep center, where your breathing, brain activity, and other vital signs are monitored. Based on the results, a healthcare professional can then determine the best treatment options, which may include continuous positive airway pressure (CPAP) therapy or oral appliances.

Seeking professional help is particularly crucial because chronic sleep disorders can have a significant impact on our daily lives. Lack of quality sleep can lead to decreased cognitive function, impaired memory, mood disorders, and increased risk of accidents. By addressing these issues with the help of a professional, we can regain control over our sleep and improve our overall health and well-being.

It's also important to remember that sleep disorders can often be interconnected with other health conditions. Seeking professional help can help identify and address any underlying medical issues that may be contributing to poor sleep. By taking a holistic approach to our sleep health, we can achieve optimal sleep and performance in all aspects of our lives.

In conclusion, seeking professional help for chronic sleep disorders is a crucial step towards achieving optimal sleep and overall well-being. By consulting with a healthcare provider and exploring treatment options such as cognitive behavioral therapy and sleep studies, we can effectively manage these disorders and improve our quality of life. Don't let sleep disorders hold you back from experiencing the power of sleep - take the first step and seek professional help today.

Dealing with Shift Work and Jet Lag

Shift work and jet lag can significantly disrupt our sleep patterns and overall well-being. Whether you are a shift worker or a frequent traveler, it is important to understand how these factors affect our sleep and learn effective strategies to mitigate their negative impact. In this subchapter, we will delve into the challenges of shift work and jet lag, and provide you with valuable tips to help you overcome them.

Shift work, such as working night shifts or rotating shifts, can wreak havoc on our sleep schedule. Our bodies have a natural circadian rhythm that regulates our sleep-wake cycle. When we disrupt this rhythm by working during the night or irregular hours, it can lead to sleep deprivation, fatigue, and decreased performance. To combat these issues, it is essential to establish a consistent sleep routine and create a sleep-friendly environment. This includes keeping your bedroom dark, cool, and quiet, using blackout curtains or eye masks to block out sunlight, and investing in a comfortable mattress and pillows.

Jet lag, on the other hand, occurs when we travel across different time zones, causing our internal body clock to become out of sync with the local time. Symptoms of jet lag include insomnia, daytime sleepiness, and difficulty concentrating. To minimize the effects of jet lag, it is recommended to gradually adjust your sleep schedule a few days before traveling, staying hydrated, and exposing yourself to natural sunlight during the day. Additionally, avoiding caffeine and alcohol before and during the flight can help regulate your sleep patterns.

In both shift work and jet lag scenarios, it is crucial to prioritize sleep and make it a non-negotiable part of your routine. Implementing relaxation techniques such as meditation, deep breathing exercises, or taking a warm bath before bed can help signal to your body that it is time to wind down and prepare for sleep. Additionally, incorporating regular exercise into your daily routine can improve sleep quality and reduce the negative effects of shift work and jet lag.

Remember, quality sleep is the key to optimal performance, no matter what type of lifestyle you lead. By understanding the challenges of shift work and jet lag and implementing these strategies, you can take control of your sleep and ultimately unlock the power of restorative rest for enhanced performance and overall well-being.

Coping with irregular work schedules

In today's fast-paced world, many individuals find themselves dealing with irregular work schedules that can greatly impact their sleep patterns and overall well-being. Whether you work night shifts, rotating shifts, or have an unpredictable work schedule, it is important to understand how to cope with these challenges and prioritize getting optimal sleep for improved performance and overall health.

One of the first steps in coping with irregular work schedules is to establish a consistent sleep routine. While this may seem challenging when your work hours vary, it is essential to create a sleep schedule that aligns with your body's natural circadian rhythm. Try to go to bed and wake up at the same time every day, even on your days off. This consistency helps regulate your body clock and ensures better quality sleep.

Creating a sleep-friendly environment is another crucial aspect of coping with irregular work schedules. Invest in blackout curtains or wear an eye mask to block out sunlight when you need to sleep during the daytime. Use earplugs or a white noise machine to drown out noise disturbances. Additionally, make your bedroom a peaceful and relaxing sanctuary by keeping it cool, clutter-free, and free from electronic devices. These measures will help promote a restful sleep environment regardless of the time you go to bed.

Managing your exposure to light is also essential for those with irregular work schedules. During the day, expose yourself to bright light to keep your body alert and awake. Conversely, when it is time to wind down and sleep, minimize your exposure to bright lights, especially from electronic devices, as they can interfere with your body's natural melatonin production, making it harder to fall asleep.

Lastly, prioritize self-care and stress management techniques to cope with the demands of an irregular work schedule. Engage in regular exercise, eat a balanced diet, and practice relaxation techniques such as meditation or deep breathing exercises. These activities help reduce stress levels and promote better sleep quality.

Remember, coping with irregular work schedules requires a proactive approach to ensure optimal sleep and performance. By establishing a consistent sleep routine, creating a sleep-friendly environment, managing light exposure, and prioritizing self-care, you can improve your sleep habits and overall well-being, even in the face of irregular work schedules. Your sleep is a powerful tool that, when optimized, can unlock your full potential in all areas of life.

Strategies to minimize the impact of shift work on sleep

Shift work is a reality for many individuals across various industries. It can significantly disrupt the natural sleep-wake cycle, leading to sleep deprivation and a range of negative health effects. However, there are strategies that can help minimize the impact of shift work on sleep and promote better overall health and performance. In this subchapter, we will explore some effective strategies that can be implemented by anyone facing the challenges of shift work.

1. Establish a Consistent Sleep Schedule: Despite the irregular working hours, try to establish a regular sleep schedule. Consistency is key to maintaining a healthy sleep routine. Set a fixed time to go to bed and wake up, even on days off. This helps regulate the body's internal clock and promotes better quality sleep.

2. Create a Sleep-friendly Environment: Make your bedroom conducive to sleep. Ensure it is dark, quiet, and at a comfortable temperature. Use blackout curtains, earplugs, or white noise machines to create a peaceful environment that supports uninterrupted sleep.

3. Prioritize Sleep Hygiene: Adopt good sleep hygiene practices to enhance sleep quality. Avoid stimulants like caffeine and nicotine close to bedtime, limit exposure to bright screens, and engage in relaxing activities before sleep, such as reading or taking a warm bath.

4. Plan Strategic Napping: Napping can help combat fatigue and increase alertness during shift work. However, it's important to plan naps strategically. Keep them short (around 20-30 minutes) and avoid taking them too close to bedtime to prevent disruption of nighttime sleep.

5. Optimize Nutrition and Exercise: Eating a balanced diet and engaging in regular physical activity can improve sleep quality. Avoid heavy meals close to bedtime and aim for regular exercise sessions, even if they need to be adjusted to fit your work schedule.

6. Seek Social Support: It can be challenging to manage the impact of shift work on sleep alone. Seek support from family, friends, or colleagues who understand the unique challenges you face. Share your experiences and concerns, and learn from others who have successfully navigated shift work.

By implementing these strategies, anyone working shifts can minimize the negative impact on their sleep and overall health. Remember, sleep is a powerful tool that can enhance performance, mental clarity, and overall well-being. Prioritizing sleep and taking proactive steps to optimize it can unlock the secrets to optimal sleep and performance, even in the face of shift work.

Managing jet lag and adjusting to new time zones

Traveling to different time zones can be an exciting adventure, but it also comes with the challenge of dealing with jet lag. Jet lag occurs when your body's internal clock, also known as the circadian rhythm, is disrupted due to crossing time zones rapidly. This disruption can lead to symptoms such as fatigue, insomnia, difficulty concentrating, and even digestive issues. However, with a few simple strategies, you can effectively manage jet lag and adjust to new time zones, ensuring that you make the most of your travels and maintain optimal sleep and performance.

One of the most effective ways to combat jet lag is by gradually adjusting your sleep schedule a few days before your trip. If you're traveling east, try going to bed and waking up earlier each day leading up to your departure. Conversely, if you're heading west, gradually shift your bedtime and wake-up time later. By doing so, your body can slowly adapt to the new time zone, minimizing the impact of jet lag.

During the flight, it's crucial to stay hydrated and avoid excessive caffeine and alcohol consumption. Dehydration can exacerbate jet lag symptoms, so drink plenty of water throughout the journey. It's also helpful to adjust your watch to the destination's time zone as soon as you board the plane. This mental shift can prepare your mind for the upcoming time adjustment, making it easier to acclimate once you arrive.

Upon arrival, try to expose yourself to natural light during the day. Natural light is a powerful tool for regulating your body's internal clock. Spend time outside, take a walk, or sit near a window to soak up the sunlight. This exposure can help reset your circadian rhythm and promote a smoother transition to the new time zone.

Establishing a regular sleep routine is essential for managing jet lag. Aim to go to bed and wake up at the same time every day, even if you're still adjusting to the new time zone. This consistency will signal your body when it's time to sleep and when it's time to wake up. Additionally, it's crucial to create a sleep-friendly environment, ensuring that your sleeping area is dark, quiet, and comfortable.

Lastly, consider using natural sleep aids such as melatonin supplements or relaxing essential oils to help regulate your sleep cycle. These can be particularly useful during the first few nights in a new time zone, as they can promote relaxation and improve sleep quality.

By implementing these strategies, you can effectively manage jet lag and adjust to new time zones with ease. Remember, getting quality sleep is essential for optimal performance, and by prioritizing your sleep, you can make the most out of your travels and enjoy every moment to the fullest.

Addressing Sleep Disturbances and Restless Nights

Sleep disturbances and restless nights can be incredibly frustrating, leaving us feeling groggy, irritable, and unable to perform at our best. In this chapter, we will explore effective strategies and techniques to address these issues and unlock the secrets to optimal sleep and performance.

One common cause of sleep disturbances is an irregular sleep schedule. Our bodies thrive on routine, so it's important to establish a consistent sleep-wake cycle. Try going to bed and waking up at the same time every day, even on weekends. This consistency will signal your body when it's time to sleep and help regulate your internal clock.

Another factor that can disrupt sleep is exposure to blue light from electronic devices. The blue light emitted by smartphones, tablets, and computers can suppress the production of melatonin, a hormone that regulates sleep. To combat this, consider setting a digital curfew and avoiding screens for at least an hour before bedtime. Instead, engage in relaxing activities such as reading a book or practicing mindfulness.

Creating a sleep-friendly environment is also crucial for addressing sleep disturbances. Ensure your bedroom is cool, dark, and quiet. Use blackout curtains or an eye mask to block out any unwanted light, and consider using earplugs or a white noise machine to drown out any disruptive sounds. Additionally, investing in a supportive mattress and comfortable pillows can make a world of difference in promoting a good night's sleep.

If you find yourself tossing and turning at night, it may be helpful to establish a bedtime routine to signal to your body that it's time to wind down. This can include activities such as taking a warm bath, practicing relaxation techniques like deep breathing or meditation, or sipping on a cup of herbal tea. Experiment with different rituals until you find what works best for you.

Finally, if sleep disturbances persist, it may be beneficial to seek professional help. Sleep disorders such as insomnia, sleep apnea, or restless leg syndrome can significantly impact your sleep quality and overall well-being. Consult with a healthcare provider who specializes in sleep medicine to determine the underlying cause of your sleep disturbances and develop a personalized treatment plan.

By addressing sleep disturbances and adopting healthier sleep habits, you can unlock the power of sleep and reap the benefits of improved cognitive function, enhanced mood, and increased productivity. Remember, quality sleep is an essential pillar of optimal health and performance.

Dealing with nightmares and night terrors

Nightmares and night terrors can be an incredibly distressing experience that can leave us feeling fearful, anxious, and exhausted. Whether you are a child or an adult, these sleep disturbances can disrupt our overall well-being and hinder our performance during the day. In this subchapter, we will explore effective strategies to deal with nightmares and night terrors, allowing you to regain control over your sleep and experience optimal rest.

Firstly, it is important to understand the difference between nightmares and night terrors. Nightmares are vivid and disturbing dreams that occur during REM (Rapid Eye Movement) sleep, typically towards the end of the night. On the other hand, night terrors are intense episodes of fear or terror that occur during non-REM sleep, usually within the first few hours of falling asleep. Recognizing the nature of these experiences can help us approach them more effectively.

One crucial step in dealing with nightmares and night terrors is to establish a consistent bedtime routine. Creating a relaxing environment before sleep, such as dimming the lights, engaging in calming activities like reading or listening to soothing music, can help reduce the likelihood of these disruptive episodes. Additionally, practicing relaxation techniques such as deep breathing or meditation before bed can alleviate anxiety and promote a peaceful sleep environment.

If nightmares persist, it may be beneficial to keep a dream journal. Recording your dreams in detail can help identify patterns, triggers, and underlying emotions associated with these episodes. By understanding the root causes of your nightmares, you can work towards resolving any underlying emotional stressors that may be contributing to their occurrence.

For children experiencing night terrors, it is essential to provide reassurance and a safe environment during these episodes. Avoid waking them abruptly, as this can increase their confusion and distress. Instead, gently guide them back to bed, ensuring their safety without fully waking them up.

In severe cases where nightmares or night terrors significantly impact your quality of life, seeking professional help from a sleep specialist or therapist may be beneficial. They can provide personalized guidance and recommend therapies such as cognitive-behavioral therapy or medication if necessary.

Remember, dealing with nightmares and night terrors is a process that requires patience and persistence. By implementing these strategies and seeking appropriate support when needed, you can reclaim restful nights and unlock the full potential of a revitalizing sleep routine.

Managing restless leg syndrome and leg cramps

Restless Leg Syndrome (RLS) and leg cramps are two common sleep disturbances that can significantly impact the quality of your sleep. These conditions can cause discomfort and restlessness in your legs, making it difficult to relax and fall asleep. In this chapter, we will discuss effective strategies to manage and alleviate the symptoms of RLS and leg cramps, allowing you to achieve a more restful and rejuvenating sleep.

Restless Leg Syndrome is characterized by an irresistible urge to move your legs, often accompanied by uncomfortable sensations such as tingling, crawling, or itching. These sensations typically worsen during periods of inactivity or at night, making it challenging to get a good night's sleep. To manage RLS, it is crucial to identify and address any underlying causes. Certain medications, vitamin deficiencies, and chronic diseases like diabetes and kidney failure can contribute to RLS symptoms. Consulting with a healthcare professional to identify and treat these underlying issues is essential for effectively managing RLS.

In addition to addressing the root cause, there are several lifestyle changes and strategies that can help alleviate RLS symptoms. Regular exercise, particularly activities that promote leg movement, such as walking or cycling, can significantly reduce symptoms. Stretching exercises, warm baths, and massages can also provide relief. Additionally, avoiding caffeine, nicotine, and alcohol, especially in the evening, can help minimize symptoms and improve overall sleep quality.

Leg cramps, on the other hand, are characterized by sudden and painful muscle contractions, often occurring during sleep. These cramps can be caused by dehydration, electrolyte imbalances, muscle fatigue, or certain medications. To manage leg cramps, it is essential to maintain proper hydration by drinking enough water throughout the day. Stretching exercises, particularly before bedtime, can help relax the muscles and prevent cramps. Massaging the affected area and applying heat packs can also provide relief.

Incorporating certain dietary changes can also be beneficial in managing leg cramps. Ensuring an adequate intake of magnesium, potassium, and calcium, either through diet or supplements, can help prevent muscle cramps. Foods rich in these minerals include bananas, leafy greens, nuts, and dairy products.

By implementing these strategies and making necessary lifestyle changes, you can effectively manage restless leg syndrome and leg cramps, ensuring a more restful and rejuvenating sleep. Remember, it is essential to consult with a healthcare professional for a proper diagnosis and personalized treatment plan. Sleep well and wake up refreshed!

Solutions for sleep disturbances caused by partner or environment

In our quest to achieve optimal sleep and performance, it is crucial to address the various factors that can disrupt our sleep patterns. One common cause of sleep disturbances is the presence of a partner or unfavorable sleeping environment. However, fear not! There are several solutions and strategies you can employ to overcome these challenges and reclaim your precious sleep.

1. Communication is key: If your partner's sleep habits are interfering with your own, it's important to have an open and honest conversation. Discuss your concerns and explore potential compromises that can accommodate both of your needs. This may involve adjusting bedtimes, finding separate sleeping spaces, or investing in a larger, more comfortable mattress.

2. Noise reduction techniques: A noisy environment can severely impact the quality of your sleep. Consider using earplugs or investing in a white noise machine to drown out disruptive sounds. Alternatively, you can try using a fan or soothing music to create a calming atmosphere that promotes restful sleep.

3. Light control: Light plays a significant role in regulating our sleep-wake cycle. If your partner's late-night reading or screen time is keeping you awake, implement light control measures. Consider using blackout curtains, eye shades, or sleep masks to create a dark environment conducive to sleep.

4. Temperature regulation: A bedroom that is too hot or too cold can make it challenging to fall asleep and stay asleep. Find a temperature that works for both you and your partner, and consider using fans,

heaters, or adjustable bedding to maintain a comfortable sleep environment.

5. Creating a sleep sanctuary: Transform your bedroom into a sleep sanctuary by eliminating clutter, creating a calming color scheme, and using comfortable bedding. Designate your bedroom as a space solely for sleep and relaxation, helping to separate it from other activities that might interfere with restful sleep.

Remember, it's essential to prioritize your sleep for optimal performance and overall well-being. By addressing and finding solutions to sleep disturbances caused by a partner or unfavorable environment, you can take control of your sleep and unlock the power of restful nights. Sweet dreams!

Chapter 4: Maximizing Performance through Optimal Sleep

Sleep for Enhanced Cognitive Function

In today's fast-paced world, where productivity and performance are highly valued, it is crucial to recognize the power of sleep in optimizing cognitive function. Sleep is not just a time for our bodies to rest and rejuvenate; it is also a period when our brains consolidate memories, process information, and recharge for the next day. In this subchapter, we delve into the importance of sleep for enhanced cognitive function, providing valuable insights and practical tips to unlock the secrets of optimal sleep and performance.

Research consistently shows that getting enough sleep is directly linked to improved cognitive abilities. During sleep, our brains go through various stages that contribute to memory consolidation, creativity, problem-solving, and attention span. By understanding and harnessing these processes, we can leverage the power of sleep to enhance our cognitive function.

One of the key mechanisms through which sleep enhances cognitive abilities is through the strengthening of neural connections. During sleep, the brain forms new connections and reinforces existing ones, leading to improved learning and memory retention. Additionally, sleep is essential for clearing out metabolic waste products that accumulate in the brain throughout the day, improving overall brain health and function.

To optimize cognitive function through sleep, it is important to prioritize sleep quality and quantity. Establishing a consistent sleep schedule, creating a conducive sleep environment, and practicing relaxation techniques before bed are all effective strategies. Furthermore, avoiding blue light exposure from electronic devices and incorporating regular exercise into your routine can also positively impact sleep quality and cognitive function.

It is worth noting that sleep deprivation can have detrimental effects on cognitive function. Chronic lack of sleep has been associated with impaired attention, memory deficits, reduced creativity, and decreased problem-solving abilities. In contrast, getting sufficient sleep can improve focus, decision-making skills, and overall cognitive performance.

In conclusion, sleep is a powerful tool for enhancing cognitive function. By recognizing the importance of sleep and implementing strategies to improve sleep quality and quantity, we can unlock the secrets to optimal sleep and performance. Prioritizing sleep will not only lead to improved cognitive abilities but also positively impact various aspects of our lives, including productivity, creativity, and overall well-being. So, let us embrace the power of sleep and unlock our full cognitive potential.

How sleep impacts memory and learning

Sleep is often overlooked as a crucial factor in our overall health and well-being. Most people understand that a good night's sleep can leave them feeling refreshed and energized the next day, but did you know that sleep also has a profound impact on memory and learning?

In this subchapter, we will explore the fascinating connection between sleep, memory, and learning. Understanding how sleep affects our cognitive abilities can empower us to make better choices when it comes to optimizing our sleep habits.

When we sleep, our brains go through different stages, including rapid eye movement (REM) sleep and non-rapid eye movement (NREM) sleep. These stages play a vital role in memory formation and consolidation. During REM sleep, our brains are highly active, processing emotions and consolidating memories, particularly those related to procedural tasks and creative problem-solving. On the other hand, NREM sleep, which includes deep sleep, is responsible for the consolidation of declarative memories, such as facts and information.

Research has shown that a lack of sleep can have a detrimental effect on memory and learning. When we don't get enough sleep, our ability to focus, concentrate, and retain information is compromised. Sleep deprivation impairs our working memory, making it harder to process and organize information effectively. It also affects our ability to form new memories and retrieve previously learned information.

Furthermore, sleep plays a crucial role in memory consolidation. During sleep, our brains replay and strengthen the neural connections formed while learning new information. This process solidifies memories, making them more resistant to forgetting. Without sufficient sleep, this consolidation process is disrupted, leading to difficulties in retaining and recalling information.

To optimize memory and learning, it is essential to prioritize quality sleep. Establishing a consistent sleep schedule, creating a conducive sleep environment, and practicing relaxation techniques before bed can greatly improve the quality and quantity of your sleep. Additionally, avoiding stimulants like caffeine and electronics before bedtime can help promote a more restful sleep.

In conclusion, sleep is not just a period of rest; it is a critical process that impacts our memory and learning abilities. By understanding and prioritizing our sleep habits, we can unlock the full potential of our cognitive abilities. Getting enough high-quality sleep is key to optimizing our memory, learning, and overall performance in all aspects of life.

Techniques to improve cognitive performance through sleep

In today's fast-paced world, where productivity and performance are highly valued, it is crucial to recognize the power of sleep in enhancing cognitive performance. Sleep is not just a period of rest; it is a restorative process that fuels our brain and helps us function optimally. In this subchapter, we will explore techniques that can improve cognitive performance through quality sleep.

First and foremost, establishing a consistent sleep routine is essential. Going to bed and waking up at the same time every day helps regulate the body's internal clock, known as the circadian rhythm. This consistency trains the body to be more alert during the day and promotes better sleep quality at night, leading to enhanced cognitive function.

Creating a sleep-friendly environment is another technique to improve cognitive performance. This includes keeping the bedroom dark, quiet, and cool. Using blackout curtains, earplugs, or white noise machines can help eliminate distractions and promote deep sleep. Additionally, investing in a comfortable mattress and pillow that suit your personal preferences can significantly enhance sleep quality.

Managing stress is crucial for optimal cognitive performance. High levels of stress can disrupt sleep patterns and impair cognitive function. Engaging in stress-reducing activities such as meditation, deep breathing exercises, or yoga before bedtime can help calm the mind and promote better sleep.

Avoiding stimulating substances like caffeine, nicotine, and alcohol close to bedtime is essential. These substances can interfere with the quality of sleep and disrupt the sleep cycle, leading to impaired cognitive performance the next day. It is advisable to avoid consuming these substances at least four to six hours before bedtime.

Lastly, incorporating regular exercise into your daily routine can have a profound impact on cognitive performance during sleep. Exercise promotes better sleep by reducing anxiety, improving mood, and increasing the amount of deep sleep experienced. Engaging in moderate-intensity exercises, such as brisk walking or cycling, for at least 30 minutes a day can significantly improve sleep quality and cognitive function.

In conclusion, improving cognitive performance through sleep requires adopting healthy sleep habits and prioritizing quality rest. By establishing a consistent sleep routine, creating a sleep-friendly environment, managing stress, avoiding stimulating substances, and incorporating regular exercise, anyone can unlock the secrets to optimal sleep and enhanced cognitive performance. Embracing the power of sleep is the key to achieving peak performance in all areas of life.

The role of sleep in enhancing focus and attention

The role of sleep in enhancing focus and attention is a crucial aspect of our overall well-being. In today's fast-paced world, where we are constantly bombarded with information and distractions, it becomes increasingly important to prioritize quality sleep to maintain optimal cognitive function. In this subchapter, we will delve into the profound impact that sleep has on our ability to stay focused and attentive, and how it can significantly improve our performance in all areas of life.

When we sleep, our brain undergoes a complex process of restoration and consolidation. During this time, our brain cells repair and regenerate, and important memories and information are solidified. This process is essential for enhancing focus and attention, as it allows our brain to filter out unnecessary information and retain what is important. Without adequate sleep, our ability to concentrate and stay attentive becomes compromised.

Research has consistently shown that sleep deprivation leads to decreased cognitive performance, including impaired attention, memory, and problem-solving skills. Lack of sleep not only affects our ability to focus on tasks, but it also hampers our decision-making abilities and creativity. Moreover, chronic sleep deprivation is linked to an increased risk of developing disorders such as attention deficit hyperactivity disorder (ADHD) and cognitive decline in the long term.

On the other hand, getting enough high-quality sleep has been proven to enhance focus and attention span. When we prioritize sleep, we are more likely to experience improved cognitive function, increased alertness, and better problem-solving skills. Additionally, a well-rested mind is better equipped to handle stress and regulate emotions, allowing us to maintain focus even in challenging situations.

To optimize sleep for enhanced focus and attention, it is important to establish a consistent sleep routine, create a sleep-friendly environment, and practice good sleep hygiene. This includes avoiding stimulating activities before bed, keeping a regular sleep schedule, and ensuring a comfortable sleep environment. Additionally, incorporating relaxation techniques such as meditation or deep breathing exercises can help calm the mind and prepare it for a restful night's sleep.

In conclusion, the role of sleep in enhancing focus and attention is undeniable. By understanding the importance of sleep and prioritizing it in our daily lives, we can unlock the secrets to optimal sleep and performance. A well-rested mind is a focused mind, capable of achieving greatness in all areas of life. So let us embrace the power of sleep and watch as our ability to concentrate and stay attentive reaches new heights.

Sleep for Physical Performance and Recovery

Sleep is not just a luxury or a way to recharge; it is an essential component of optimal physical performance and recovery. In this subchapter, we will explore the profound impact that sleep has on our physical abilities and how prioritizing quality sleep can unlock our full potential.

When it comes to physical performance, sleep is a game-changer. Research has consistently shown that getting enough sleep improves athletic performance, reaction time, and coordination. In fact, studies have demonstrated that sleep deprivation can have similar effects on the body as alcohol intoxication, impairing judgment and motor skills. Simply put, if you want to excel in any physical activity, whether it's running, weightlifting, or even everyday tasks, sleep is your secret weapon.

But it's not just about performing better; sleep is also crucial for recovery. During sleep, our bodies undergo essential repair processes, including muscle growth and tissue regeneration. Without adequate sleep, these processes are disrupted, leading to slower recovery times and increased risk of injuries. Additionally, lack of sleep can lead to higher levels of inflammation in the body, which can hinder recovery and increase the likelihood of chronic conditions such as heart disease and diabetes.

To optimize physical performance and recovery through sleep, there are a few key strategies to consider. First and foremost, prioritize quantity and quality. Aim for at least seven to nine hours of uninterrupted sleep every night, ensuring you create a sleep-friendly environment that is cool, dark, and quiet. Establishing a consistent bedtime routine can also signal your body that it's time to wind down and prepare for sleep.

Another essential aspect is managing stress and promoting relaxation before sleep. Engaging in activities such as meditation, deep breathing exercises, or gentle stretching can help calm the mind and body, setting the stage for a restful night's sleep.

Lastly, pay attention to your sleep hygiene. This includes avoiding stimulants like caffeine and electronic devices close to bedtime, as they can interfere with your ability to fall asleep and stay asleep.

By understanding the power of sleep for physical performance and recovery, you can unlock your full potential in any physical activity. Whether you are an athlete, a fitness enthusiast, or simply someone who wants to improve their overall health, prioritizing sleep will undoubtedly enhance your performance and help you achieve your goals. So, make sleep a non-negotiable part of your routine, and reap the incredible benefits it has to offer.

The Importance of Sleep in Muscle Recovery and Growth

Introduction:

In this subchapter, we will explore the vital role that sleep plays in muscle recovery and growth. Whether you are an athlete looking to enhance your performance, a fitness enthusiast striving to reach your goals, or simply someone interested in optimizing your overall health, understanding the power of sleep in muscle recovery is crucial. Sleep is not just a period of rest; it is a time when your body undergoes essential processes that promote muscle repair, growth, and overall well-being.

The Science Behind Muscle Recovery:

Muscle recovery is a complex process that involves the repair of microscopic muscle damage caused during physical activity. When you engage in intense exercise, your muscle fibers experience tiny tears and breakdown. Through a process called protein synthesis, these damaged muscle fibers are rebuilt, resulting in stronger, more resilient muscles. However, without adequate sleep, this recovery process is compromised.

Sleep and Hormonal Balance:

One of the key mechanisms by which sleep aids muscle recovery is through the regulation of hormones. During sleep, your body produces growth hormone, which is essential for muscle growth and repair. Additionally, sleep helps balance other hormones such as cortisol, which is known as the stress hormone. High levels of cortisol can impede muscle recovery and hinder growth. By getting sufficient sleep, you can maintain a healthy hormonal balance, optimizing your body's ability to repair and build muscle.

Quality and Quantity of Sleep:

Both the quality and quantity of sleep play significant roles in muscle recovery and growth. It is not just about the number of hours you sleep; the quality of your sleep matters too. Deep, restorative sleep is essential for muscle repair. During deep sleep stages, your body releases human growth hormone (HGH), which stimulates tissue growth and repair. This is why it is crucial to prioritize both the duration and the quality of your sleep to maximize muscle recovery.

Sleep Hygiene Tips for Optimal Muscle Recovery:

To ensure that you are getting the most out of your sleep for muscle recovery and growth, it is important to practice good sleep hygiene. This includes maintaining a consistent sleep schedule, creating a comfortable sleep environment, avoiding stimulants like caffeine before bed, and implementing relaxation techniques such as meditation or deep breathing exercises. By incorporating these habits into your routine, you can improve the quality and duration of your sleep, thereby enhancing muscle recovery and growth.

Conclusion:

In conclusion, sleep is a powerful tool for muscle recovery and growth. By understanding the science behind muscle repair, the role of hormones, and the importance of both quality and quantity of sleep, you can harness the power of sleep to optimize your athletic performance, fitness goals, and overall well-being. Prioritize sleep as an integral part of your muscle recovery routine, and you will reap the benefits of stronger, healthier muscles and improved physical performance.

Sleep's impact on athletic performance and injury prevention

A good night's sleep is crucial for maintaining optimal performance in any athletic endeavor. Whether you are a professional athlete or simply enjoy participating in recreational sports, understanding the relationship between sleep and athletic performance can greatly enhance your abilities and prevent injuries. In this subchapter, we will explore the profound impact that sleep has on athletic performance and injury prevention.

Athletes who prioritize sleep consistently outperform those who neglect it. During sleep, the body undergoes essential processes such as muscle repair and growth, hormone regulation, and memory consolidation. These processes are vital for athletes as they contribute to muscle recovery, increased strength, and improved coordination. Without adequate sleep, these benefits become compromised, leading to decreased performance on the field or court.

Furthermore, sleep plays a significant role in injury prevention. Fatigue resulting from inadequate sleep can impair an athlete's judgment, reaction time, and coordination, making them more susceptible to accidents and injuries. Sleep deprivation has also been linked to decreased pain tolerance, further increasing the risk of injury. By prioritizing sleep, athletes can reduce the likelihood of accidents and maintain their physical well-being.

In addition to quantity, the quality of sleep is equally important for athletes. Deep sleep, also known as slow-wave sleep, is the stage where the body experiences the most restorative effects. This is when the body repairs damaged tissues, strengthens the immune system, and releases growth hormones. Athletes should aim to achieve quality sleep by creating a conducive sleep environment, adopting relaxation techniques, and establishing a consistent sleep routine.

It is worth noting that sleep is not only beneficial for physical performance but also cognitive function. Sleep deprivation can impair decision-making abilities, attention, and reaction time, negatively affecting an athlete's overall performance. By prioritizing sleep, athletes can enhance their mental acuity, enabling them to make quick and accurate decisions during critical moments in a game or competition.

In conclusion, sleep plays a vital role in athletic performance and injury prevention. By understanding the profound impact that sleep has on the body's restorative processes, athletes can unlock their true potential and reduce the risk of injuries. Prioritizing both quantity and quality of sleep is essential for optimal performance in any athletic endeavor. So, whether you are a professional athlete or a recreational sports enthusiast, make sleep a top priority and watch your athletic abilities soar to new heights.

Strategies for optimizing sleep to improve physical abilities

Sleep is a fundamental aspect of our lives that plays a crucial role in our overall health and well-being. It is during sleep that our bodies repair, regenerate, and strengthen themselves, allowing us to perform at our best physically and mentally. In this subchapter, we will explore strategies for optimizing sleep to improve physical abilities, helping you harness the power of sleep for enhanced performance.

Firstly, it is essential to establish a consistent sleep schedule. Going to bed and waking up at the same time every day, even on weekends, helps regulate your body's internal clock, promoting better sleep quality. This consistency allows your body to optimize the release of hormones, such as melatonin, which aids in falling asleep and maintaining a deep sleep state.

Creating a sleep-friendly environment is another crucial strategy. Your bedroom should be cool, quiet, and dark to promote relaxation and minimize disruptions. Investing in a comfortable mattress and pillow that support your body's natural alignment can significantly improve your sleep quality.

Limiting exposure to technology before bed is essential for optimizing sleep. The blue light emitted by electronic devices, such as smartphones and tablets, can suppress the production of melatonin, making it harder to fall asleep. Establish a technology curfew at least an hour before bedtime and engage in relaxing activities instead, such as reading a book or practicing meditation.

Implementing a pre-sleep routine can help signal to your body that it is time to wind down. This routine can include activities such as taking a warm bath, practicing gentle stretching or yoga, or listening to calming music. These activities can help relax your mind and body, preparing you for a restful night's sleep.

Lastly, paying attention to your diet and exercise habits can significantly impact your sleep quality and physical abilities. Avoid consuming large meals, caffeine, or alcohol close to bedtime, as they can interfere with your sleep patterns. Regular exercise, on the other hand, can promote better sleep by reducing stress and anxiety and increasing your body's need for restorative sleep.

By implementing these strategies for optimizing sleep, you can unlock the secrets to optimal sleep and performance. Remember, quality sleep is not a luxury; it is a necessity for peak physical abilities. So, prioritize your sleep and unlock the power it holds for your overall well-being and success.

Sleep for Emotional Well-being and Mental Health

In today's fast-paced world, it's easy to overlook the importance of sleep when it comes to our emotional well-being and mental health. We often prioritize other aspects of our lives, such as work or social obligations, over getting a good night's sleep. However, research has shown that sleep plays a crucial role in our overall mental and emotional well-being.

Sleep is not just a time for our bodies to rest; it is also a time for our minds to process and consolidate information. During sleep, our brains go through various stages that help regulate our emotions and support mental health. When we don't get enough sleep, this delicate balance is disrupted, leading to a range of emotional and mental health issues.

One of the key ways that sleep affects our emotional well-being is through its impact on stress levels. Lack of sleep can make us more vulnerable to stress, increasing our chances of experiencing anxiety and depression. When we are sleep-deprived, our brains become more reactive to negative stimuli, making it harder for us to regulate our emotions effectively. This can lead to mood swings, irritability, and difficulty coping with daily challenges.

Moreover, sleep deprivation has been linked to an increased risk of developing mental health disorders such as bipolar disorder and schizophrenia. It can also worsen the symptoms of existing conditions, making it harder to manage them effectively. Sleep is essential for maintaining the brain's chemical balance, and when this balance is disrupted, it can have a profound impact on our mental health.

On the other hand, prioritizing sleep and getting enough restful hours can have a positive impact on our emotional well-being. Quality sleep helps regulate our emotions, improve our mood, and enhance our ability to cope with stress. It also allows us to have greater clarity of thought, improved focus, and better decision-making skills.

To ensure optimal sleep for emotional well-being and mental health, it's important to establish a consistent sleep routine. This includes going to bed and waking up at the same time every day, creating a sleep-friendly environment, and practicing relaxation techniques before bed. Avoiding stimulants such as caffeine and electronic devices before bedtime can also significantly improve sleep quality.

In conclusion, sleep plays a vital role in our emotional well-being and mental health. By prioritizing and optimizing our sleep habits, we can improve our ability to cope with stress, regulate our emotions effectively, and maintain good mental health. Don't underestimate the power of sleep in unlocking your full potential and achieving optimal performance in all areas of life.

The relationship between sleep and mental health

The relationship between sleep and mental health is an essential aspect of our overall well-being. In this subchapter, we will explore the profound impact that sleep has on our mental health, and how prioritizing quality sleep can significantly improve various aspects of our lives.

Sleep is not merely a time when our bodies rest; it is also a crucial period for our brains to rejuvenate and recharge. Research has consistently shown that lack of sleep or poor sleep quality can lead to an array of mental health issues, including depression, anxiety, and mood disorders. When we don't get enough sleep, our cognitive function becomes impaired, making it difficult to concentrate, remember information, and make rational decisions. These cognitive deficits can further contribute to the development of mental health disorders.

Furthermore, the relationship between sleep and mental health is bidirectional. Meaning that not only does poor sleep contribute to mental health issues, but mental health problems can also disrupt our sleep patterns. Conditions such as depression and anxiety often lead to insomnia or disrupted sleep, creating a vicious cycle where poor sleep exacerbates mental health issues, and mental health issues, in turn, disturb sleep.

Understanding this relationship is crucial because it highlights the importance of taking steps to improve our sleep habits for the sake of our mental well-being. By prioritizing quality sleep, we can enhance our mood, reduce stress, and increase resilience to life's challenges. Quality sleep allows our brains to process emotions and experiences effectively, leading to improved mental clarity and a more positive outlook on life.

In this subchapter, we will delve into practical strategies for optimizing sleep to improve mental health. We will explore the power of establishing a consistent sleep routine, creating a sleep-friendly environment, and incorporating relaxation techniques before bed. Additionally, we will discuss the benefits of regular exercise, the impact of nutrition on sleep, and the role of technology in disrupting our sleep patterns.

By incorporating these strategies into our daily lives, we can unlock the secrets to optimal sleep and performance. Whether you are struggling with mental health issues or simply seeking to enhance your overall well-being, understanding the relationship between sleep and mental health is the first step towards achieving a healthier, more balanced life. Join us as we delve into the power of sleep and discover the transformative potential it holds for our mental well-being.

Sleep's effect on mood regulation and emotional resilience

Sleep Smarter: Unlocking the Secrets to Optimal Sleep and Performance

Introduction:

In our fast-paced world, sleep is often seen as a luxury rather than a necessity. We stay up late, scrolling through social media or binge-watching our favorite shows, sacrificing precious hours of sleep. However, what many people fail to realize is that sleep plays a crucial role in regulating our mood and enhancing our emotional resilience. In this subchapter, we will explore the fascinating connection between sleep and our emotional well-being.

The Impact of Sleep on Mood Regulation:

Have you ever noticed how a poor night's sleep can leave you feeling irritable and moody the next day? This is not a coincidence. Sleep deprivation disrupts the delicate balance of hormones and neurotransmitters in our brains that regulate our mood. When we don't get enough sleep, the production of serotonin, a hormone that helps regulate emotions, decreases, leading to increased feelings of irritability, anger, and sadness. Furthermore, lack of sleep also affects the brain's prefrontal cortex, responsible for rational thinking and emotional regulation, making it harder to manage our emotions effectively.

Enhancing Emotional Resilience:

Sleep is not only crucial for regulating our mood, but it also plays a vital role in building emotional resilience. Emotional resilience refers to our ability to bounce back from stressful situations and adapt to adversity. When we get enough sleep, our brains process and consolidate emotional experiences, helping us better cope with challenging circumstances. Sleep deprivation, on the other hand, impairs our ability to adapt to stress, making it more difficult to regulate emotions and respond effectively to difficult situations.

Practical Tips for Improving Sleep and Emotional Well-being:

Now that we understand the importance of sleep for mood regulation and emotional resilience, let's explore some practical tips to optimize our sleep and enhance our emotional well-being. First and foremost, prioritize sleep by establishing a consistent sleep schedule and creating a relaxing bedtime routine. Avoid caffeine and electronic devices before bed, as they can interfere with sleep quality. Additionally, create a sleep-friendly environment by ensuring your bedroom is cool, dark, and quiet.

Conclusion:

In this subchapter, we have explored the powerful connection between sleep and mood regulation, as well as emotional resilience. Sleep is not just a time for rest; it is a critical period for our brains to recharge and process emotions. By prioritizing sleep and adopting healthy sleep habits, we can unlock the secrets to optimal sleep and performance, improving our mood, and enhancing our emotional well-being. Remember, a good night's sleep is not a luxury – it is an essential ingredient for a happy and resilient life.

Improving mental well-being through quality sleep

In today's fast-paced world, we often underestimate the power of sleep and its impact on our mental well-being. We live in a society that values productivity and achievement, often sacrificing our sleep to meet the demands of our daily lives. However, prioritizing quality sleep is essential for not only our physical health but also our mental well-being.

Sleep is a vital component of our overall health, and it plays a crucial role in maintaining a balanced state of mind. When we sleep, our brain goes through various stages, each with its own purpose in supporting our mental and emotional well-being. During the deep stages of sleep, our brain consolidates memories and processes emotions, allowing us to wake up feeling refreshed and mentally rejuvenated.

Lack of quality sleep can have a significant impact on our mental health. Studies have shown that individuals who regularly experience sleep deprivation are more prone to developing mental health issues such as anxiety and depression. Sleep deprivation can disrupt the delicate balance of chemicals in our brain, affecting our mood, ability to cope with stress, and overall cognitive function.

On the other hand, getting enough quality sleep can enhance our mental well-being in numerous ways. It improves our ability to concentrate, make decisions, and solve problems effectively. A rested mind is also more resilient to stress, enabling us to cope with life's challenges more efficiently. Additionally, quality sleep promotes emotional stability, reducing the risk of mood swings and irritability.

To improve your mental well-being through quality sleep, it is crucial to prioritize sleep hygiene. Establishing a consistent sleep schedule, creating a relaxing bedtime routine, and ensuring a comfortable sleep environment are essential steps in optimizing the quality of your sleep. Avoiding stimulants such as caffeine and electronic devices close to bedtime can also contribute to better sleep quality.

Furthermore, incorporating relaxation techniques into your bedtime routine can promote better sleep and mental well-being. Deep breathing exercises, meditation, and journaling can help calm the mind and prepare it for a restful night's sleep.

Remember, sleep is not a luxury; it is a fundamental necessity for our mental well-being. By prioritizing quality sleep and making it a non-negotiable part of our daily routine, we can unlock the secrets to optimal sleep and performance, leading to a happier, healthier, and more fulfilling life.

Chapter 5: Implementing Sleep Smarter Habits

Tracking and Monitoring Sleep Patterns

In today's fast-paced world, sleep has become a luxury that many people struggle to afford. We often sacrifice our sleep to meet work deadlines, fulfill social commitments, or binge-watch our favorite shows. However, what we fail to realize is that adequate and quality sleep is the key to unlocking our true potential and improving our overall performance. In this subchapter, we will explore the importance of tracking and monitoring our sleep patterns to help us harness the power of sleep.

Tracking and monitoring sleep patterns can provide us with valuable insights into our sleep quality, duration, and efficiency. By understanding our unique sleep patterns, we can make informed decisions to optimize our sleep and wake up feeling refreshed and revitalized.

One of the most effective ways to track and monitor sleep patterns is by using sleep tracking technology. These devices, such as wearable fitness trackers or smartphone apps, can provide us with data on our sleep stages, heart rate, breathing patterns, and even the amount of time we spend in deep sleep or REM sleep. Armed with this information, we can identify any sleep disturbances, such as sleep apnea or restless leg syndrome, and take appropriate measures to address them.

Moreover, tracking our sleep patterns can help us identify lifestyle factors that may be negatively impacting our sleep. For instance, we may discover that consuming caffeine too close to bedtime, using electronic devices in bed, or having an irregular sleep schedule are disrupting our sleep. Armed with this knowledge, we can make necessary changes to create a sleep-friendly environment and establish healthy sleep habits.

Monitoring sleep patterns also enables us to evaluate the effectiveness of different sleep interventions. Whether it's trying out a new mattress, adopting a specific sleep routine, or incorporating relaxation techniques into our bedtime routine, tracking our sleep patterns allows us to assess whether these interventions are truly helping us achieve better sleep.

In conclusion, tracking and monitoring sleep patterns is a powerful tool that empowers us to take control of our sleep and enhance our performance. By understanding our unique sleep patterns, identifying sleep disturbances, and evaluating the effectiveness of various interventions, we can unlock the secrets to optimal sleep and reclaim our vitality. So, start tracking your sleep patterns today and embark on a journey towards a healthier, more fulfilling life powered by the transformative benefits of a good night's sleep.

Utilizing sleep trackers and apps for insight

In today's fast-paced world, many of us struggle to get a good night's sleep. We toss and turn, unable to quiet our minds and fall into a deep slumber. Fortunately, technology has come to our aid in the form of sleep trackers and apps that can provide valuable insights into our sleep patterns and help us optimize our sleep for better performance during the day.

Sleep trackers and apps are powerful tools that can help us understand the quality and quantity of our sleep. These devices, typically worn on the wrist or placed next to the bed, monitor various aspects of our sleep, such as the time it takes us to fall asleep, the duration of our sleep cycles, and even the quality of our REM (rapid eye movement) sleep. With this data, we can gain a deeper understanding of our sleep patterns and identify any issues that may be affecting the quality of our rest.

One of the key benefits of sleep trackers and apps is their ability to provide personalized insights. By analyzing the data collected over time, these devices can identify trends and patterns unique to each individual. For example, they may reveal that certain activities or habits, such as consuming caffeine too close to bedtime or using electronic devices before sleep, negatively impact our sleep quality. Armed with this knowledge, we can make informed decisions and implement changes to improve our sleep hygiene.

Moreover, sleep trackers and apps often come with additional features that can further enhance our sleep experience. For instance, some devices use gentle vibrations or soothing sounds to wake us up during our lightest sleep phase, ensuring we wake up feeling refreshed and energized. Others offer guided meditation or relaxation exercises to help us unwind and prepare for sleep. These features can be particularly beneficial for those who struggle with falling asleep or waking up feeling groggy.

It is important to note that while sleep trackers and apps can provide valuable insights, they should not replace professional medical advice. If you are experiencing chronic sleep issues or suspect an underlying sleep disorder, it is always recommended to consult with a healthcare professional.

In conclusion, sleep trackers and apps are powerful tools that can provide valuable insights into our sleep patterns. By utilizing these devices, we can gain a deeper understanding of our sleep quality, identify potential issues, and make informed decisions to improve our sleep hygiene. With optimized sleep, we can unlock the secrets to optimal performance and experience the true power of sleep.

Analyzing sleep data to identify patterns and areas for improvement

In today's fast-paced world, it can be easy to overlook the importance of a good night's sleep. However, sleep plays an integral role in our overall well-being, affecting our physical health, mental clarity, and cognitive performance. Understanding the power of sleep and how to optimize it can have a profound impact on our lives. One effective way to gain insights into our sleep patterns and identify areas for improvement is through analyzing sleep data.

Thanks to advancements in technology, we now have access to an array of sleep tracking devices and smartphone applications that can monitor and record our sleep patterns. These tools can provide valuable information about the duration and quality of our sleep, as well as other factors that can impact our rest, such as room temperature, noise levels, and even heart rate variability.

By collecting and analyzing sleep data over a period of time, we can identify patterns and trends that may be affecting the quality of our sleep. For example, we may discover that we consistently have trouble falling asleep on nights when we consume caffeine in the evening or when we engage in stimulating activities right before bed. Armed with this knowledge, we can make informed decisions to adjust our habits and create a sleep-friendly environment.

Analyzing sleep data can also help us identify potential sleep disorders or underlying health issues that may be impacting our sleep quality. For instance, if we consistently experience periods of snoring or pauses in breathing during sleep, it could be an indication of sleep apnea. By recognizing these patterns through data analysis, we can seek appropriate medical intervention and improve our overall sleep health.

Moreover, tracking our sleep can serve as a motivation to prioritize and improve our sleep habits. The visual representation of our sleep patterns, such as graphs and charts, can provide a tangible reminder of the importance of quality sleep. It can also highlight the positive changes we make over time, reinforcing the benefits and encouraging us to continue making improvements.

In conclusion, analyzing sleep data is a powerful tool in understanding our sleep patterns and identifying areas for improvement. By leveraging technology and monitoring our sleep, we can gain valuable insights into our sleep quality, identify potential issues, and make informed decisions to optimize our sleep. Remember, quality sleep is not a luxury; it is an essential component of overall well-being and can greatly enhance our performance in all aspects of life.

Setting goals and tracking progress towards optimal sleep

In order to harness the power of sleep and unlock its secrets for optimal performance, it is essential to set goals and track your progress. When it comes to achieving quality sleep, it is not enough to simply go to bed and hope for the best. By setting clear objectives and monitoring your sleep patterns, you can make informed choices and take proactive steps towards improving your sleep quality.

One of the first goals you should set is determining the amount of sleep your body truly needs. While the general recommendation is around 7-9 hours, it can vary from person to person. By experimenting with different sleep durations and paying attention to how you feel upon waking up, you can find your optimal sleep duration. Tracking your sleep patterns using a sleep tracker or a journal can be immensely helpful in this process.

Another goal to consider is establishing a consistent sleep schedule. Our bodies thrive on routine, so it is crucial to go to bed and wake up at the same time every day, even on weekends. This consistency helps regulate our internal body clock, making it easier to fall asleep and wake up naturally. Use an alarm clock or set reminders to ensure you stick to your sleep schedule until it becomes a habit.

Monitoring your progress is equally important in achieving optimal sleep. Keep a sleep journal where you record your sleep quality, any disturbances, and how you feel during the day. This journal can help you identify patterns and triggers that affect your sleep negatively, such as caffeine intake or evening screen time. By analyzing your journal entries, you can make adjustments and track the improvements in your sleep quality over time.

Additionally, consider using a sleep tracker or smartphone app that monitors your sleep cycles, heart rate, and movement during the night. These tools provide valuable insights into your sleep patterns and can help you identify any potential sleep disorders or disturbances that may be impacting your sleep quality.

Remember that setting goals and tracking your progress towards optimal sleep is a journey. It requires patience, consistency, and a commitment to making sleep a priority. By taking the time to understand your sleep needs, establishing a routine, and monitoring your progress, you can unlock the secrets of optimal sleep and harness its power to enhance your performance in all aspects of life.

Building a Personalized Sleep Routine

In today's fast-paced world, where everyone seems to be constantly on the go, it's easy to neglect one of the most vital aspects of our lives - sleep. However, discovering the power of sleep and incorporating it into our daily routines can have a profound impact on our overall well-being and performance. In this subchapter, we will explore the secrets to building a personalized sleep routine that will unlock the potential of optimal sleep and performance.

The first step in building a personalized sleep routine is understanding the importance of quality sleep. Sleep is not just a period of rest; it is a critical time during which our bodies repair, restore, and rejuvenate themselves. Without sufficient and restorative sleep, we become more susceptible to a host of health issues, including obesity, diabetes, and cardiovascular diseases.

To begin, it's essential to establish a consistent sleep schedule. Going to bed and waking up at the same time every day, even on weekends, helps regulate our internal body clock and optimize our sleep quality. It's also important to create a relaxing pre-sleep routine that helps signal our bodies that it's time to wind down. This routine might include activities such as reading a book, taking a warm bath, or practicing meditation.

Creating a sleep-friendly environment is another crucial aspect of building a personalized sleep routine. Keeping your bedroom cool, dark, and quiet can greatly enhance the quality of your sleep. Investing in a comfortable mattress and pillows, as well as using blackout curtains and white noise machines, can also contribute to a more restful night's sleep.

Furthermore, it's essential to pay attention to our daytime habits, as they directly influence our sleep quality. Regular exercise, preferably in the morning or early afternoon, can promote better sleep. However, engaging in vigorous exercise too close to bedtime can have a stimulating effect and make it harder to fall asleep. Additionally, limiting caffeine intake, especially in the afternoon and evening, and avoiding heavy meals or alcohol before bed can significantly improve sleep quality.

In conclusion, building a personalized sleep routine is crucial for harnessing the power of sleep and unlocking optimal performance. By understanding the importance of quality sleep, establishing a consistent sleep schedule, creating a sleep-friendly environment, and maintaining healthy daytime habits, we can transform our lives and achieve the well-rested state necessary to excel in all areas. Remember, a good night's sleep is not a luxury; it's a necessity for a healthier, happier, and more productive life.

Customizing a sleep routine based on individual preferences

In the pursuit of optimal sleep and performance, one size does not fit all. Just as each person is unique, so too are their sleep preferences. Whether you're a night owl or an early bird, it's crucial to customize your sleep routine to suit your individual needs. By understanding your own preferences and tailoring your routine accordingly, you can unlock the power of sleep and reap its numerous benefits.

First and foremost, it's essential to determine your natural circadian rhythm. This internal clock dictates your sleep-wake cycle and can vary from person to person. Some individuals thrive in the early morning hours, while others find their energy peaks in the evening. By identifying your circadian rhythm, you can align your sleep schedule accordingly, ensuring that you maximize your productivity and overall well-being.

Once you've established your natural rhythm, it's time to customize your sleep routine. This involves creating an environment conducive to quality sleep. Consider factors such as lighting, noise, and temperature. Some individuals find a dark and quiet room ideal, while others may prefer a white noise machine or a fan for background noise. Experiment with different options until you find what works best for you.

Additionally, pay attention to your pre-sleep routine. Establishing a relaxing bedtime ritual can signal to your body and mind that it's time to unwind and prepare for sleep. This could include activities such as reading a book, taking a warm bath, or practicing mindfulness meditation. Find activities that help you relax and incorporate them into your routine consistently.

Furthermore, it's crucial to prioritize sleep quantity and quality. While the recommended amount of sleep varies based on age and individual needs, it's generally advised to aim for seven to nine hours of uninterrupted sleep. However, quality is just as important as quantity. Create a sleep environment that promotes deep, restorative sleep. Invest in a comfortable mattress and pillow, and consider using blackout curtains or an eye mask to block out any unwanted light.

By customizing your sleep routine based on your individual preferences, you can harness the power of sleep to enhance your performance and overall well-being. Remember, there is no one-size-fits-all approach when it comes to sleep. Experiment, listen to your body, and make adjustments as necessary. Unlocking the secrets to optimal sleep and performance starts with understanding and respecting your unique sleep needs.

Incorporating relaxation techniques and sleep rituals

Incorporating relaxation techniques and sleep rituals is crucial for harnessing the power of sleep and optimizing both our physical and mental performance. In this subchapter, we will explore various techniques and rituals that can help you achieve a deeper and more restful sleep.

One effective relaxation technique is deep breathing. By taking slow, deep breaths and focusing on your breath, you can activate your body's relaxation response, which helps to calm the mind and prepare it for sleep. Incorporating deep breathing exercises into your bedtime routine can signal to your body that it's time to unwind and relax.

Another powerful technique is progressive muscle relaxation. This involves systematically tensing and then releasing each muscle group in your body, starting from your toes and working your way up to your head. By consciously relaxing your muscles, you can release any tension or stress that may have built up throughout the day, allowing your body to enter a state of deep relaxation.

Creating a sleep ritual is also essential for promoting optimal sleep. This can include activities such as dimming the lights, taking a warm bath, or reading a book before bed. By consistently engaging in these activities before sleep, you train your mind and body to associate them with relaxation and sleep. This helps to establish a consistent sleep schedule and can improve the quality of your sleep over time.

In addition to relaxation techniques and rituals, it's important to create a sleep-friendly environment. This includes keeping your bedroom cool, dark, and quiet. Investing in a comfortable mattress and pillows can also greatly enhance your sleep quality.

By incorporating these relaxation techniques and sleep rituals into your daily routine, you can tap into the power of sleep and unlock its secrets to optimal performance. Remember, sleep is not just a luxury but a necessity for our overall well-being. So, take the time to prioritize your sleep and reap the benefits of improved energy, focus, and overall health.

Adjusting the routine based on feedback and results

In the pursuit of optimal sleep and performance, it is crucial to understand that our bodies are not static entities. They constantly evolve and respond to the environment and stimuli around us. As such, it is imperative to adjust our routines based on feedback and results to ensure we are getting the most out of our sleep.

When it comes to the power of sleep, there is no one-size-fits-all approach. Each individual is unique, with varying needs and preferences. Therefore, it is essential to pay attention to the feedback our bodies provide and make necessary adjustments to our sleep routine.

One vital aspect to consider is the quality and duration of our sleep. By monitoring how we feel upon waking up, throughout the day, and before going to bed, we can gain valuable insights into our sleep patterns. Are we waking up feeling refreshed and energized? Or do we struggle to get out of bed, feeling groggy and fatigued? These indicators can help us determine whether our current routine is working or needs adjustment.

Additionally, tracking our sleep duration can provide valuable information. Are we consistently getting enough hours of sleep? Or are we falling short, leading to daytime sleepiness and decreased performance? By analyzing these results, we can make necessary changes, such as adjusting our bedtime or creating a more conducive sleep environment.

Furthermore, paying attention to the impact of external factors on our sleep is crucial. Are there certain habits or activities that disrupt our sleep quality? Perhaps it's excessive screen time before bed, consuming caffeine too close to bedtime, or a noisy sleeping environment. By identifying these factors and making appropriate changes, we can optimize our sleep and enhance our performance during the day.

Lastly, it is important to remember that adjusting our sleep routine based on feedback and results is an ongoing process. Our bodies and needs change over time, and what once worked may no longer be effective. By regularly assessing our sleep patterns and making necessary adjustments, we can ensure that our sleep routine continues to support our overall well-being and performance.

In conclusion, adjusting the routine based on feedback and results is a crucial aspect of harnessing the power of sleep. By paying attention to how we feel, monitoring our sleep duration, and addressing external factors, we can optimize our sleep routine for optimal performance. Remember, the key to unlocking the secrets of optimal sleep lies in our ability to adapt and adjust.

Maintaining Consistency and Sustaining Healthy Sleep Habits

In our fast-paced and hectic lives, it is essential to prioritize our sleep and develop healthy sleep habits to unlock the power of rest. Consistency is key when it comes to achieving optimal sleep and reaping its numerous benefits. In this subchapter, we will explore the importance of maintaining consistency in our sleep routine and provide practical tips to sustain healthy sleep habits.

Consistency is the foundation of quality sleep. Our bodies thrive on routine, and the same applies to our sleep patterns. By going to bed and waking up at the same time every day, we regulate our internal clock, also known as the circadian rhythm. This consistency helps synchronize our biological processes, allowing us to fall asleep faster and wake up feeling refreshed. Whether it's a weekday or weekend, try to stick to your sleep schedule as closely as possible to maintain a consistent rhythm.

Creating an ideal sleep environment is another crucial aspect of sustaining healthy sleep habits. Make sure your bedroom is dark, quiet, and cool. Invest in comfortable bedding and a supportive mattress to enhance your sleep quality. Avoid electronic devices such as smartphones or tablets before bed, as the blue light emitted can disrupt your sleep-wake cycle. Instead, engage in relaxing activities like reading or practicing meditation to wind down before sleep.

Establishing a bedtime routine can signal your body that it is time to relax and prepare for sleep. Engage in activities that promote relaxation, such as taking a warm bath, listening to soothing music, or practicing gentle stretches. Avoid stimulating substances like caffeine or nicotine close to bedtime, as they can interfere with your ability to fall asleep.

Additionally, paying attention to your diet and exercise habits can greatly impact your sleep quality. Regular exercise can improve sleep duration and quality, but avoid intense workouts close to bedtime, as they can elevate your heart rate and make it difficult to relax. Opt for a balanced diet, rich in sleep-promoting nutrients like magnesium and tryptophan, while avoiding heavy meals or spicy foods before bed.

By maintaining consistency in your sleep routine, creating a conducive sleep environment, establishing a bedtime routine, and adopting healthy lifestyle habits, you can unlock the power of sleep and optimize your performance in all areas of life. Remember, quality sleep is not a luxury; it is a necessity for your physical, mental, and emotional well-being.

Overcoming challenges and maintaining motivation

In the pursuit of optimal sleep and performance, challenges and setbacks are inevitable. However, it is important to remember that these obstacles are not insurmountable, and with the right mindset and strategies, we can overcome them and maintain our motivation to achieve our goals.

One of the most common challenges people face when trying to improve their sleep is breaking old habits and establishing new ones. Whether it's staying up late to binge-watch our favorite TV shows or relying on caffeine to power through the day, these habits can be tough to break. However, by understanding the power of sleep and the impact it has on our overall well-being, we can find the motivation to make positive changes.

To overcome these challenges, it is essential to set realistic goals and create a plan of action. Start by identifying the specific habits or behaviors that are hindering your sleep quality and performance. Then, gradually replace them with healthier alternatives. For example, if you find yourself scrolling through your phone before bed, try implementing a digital detox an hour before sleep and engaging in a relaxing activity instead, such as reading a book or practicing deep breathing exercises.

Another common challenge is dealing with external factors that disrupt our sleep, such as noise, light, or an uncomfortable sleep environment. To address these challenges, consider investing in earplugs, blackout curtains, or a comfortable mattress and pillow that promote a restful night's sleep. Creating a sleep-friendly environment can significantly improve the quality and duration of your sleep, leading to enhanced performance and overall well-being.

Additionally, maintaining motivation can be a struggle, especially when progress seems slow or setbacks occur. It is essential to remember that improving sleep is a journey, and setbacks are a natural part of the process. Instead of dwelling on setbacks, focus on the progress you have made and the positive changes you have experienced. Celebrate small victories along the way to stay motivated and build momentum.

Seeking support from others can also be instrumental in overcoming challenges and maintaining motivation. Surround yourself with like-minded individuals who understand the power of sleep and support your goals. Share your progress, seek advice, and offer support to others on a similar journey. Connecting with others who share your passion for optimal sleep can provide encouragement and accountability.

In conclusion, overcoming challenges and maintaining motivation in the pursuit of optimal sleep and performance is possible with the right mindset and strategies. By setting realistic goals, creating a plan of action, creating a sleep-friendly environment, celebrating small victories, and seeking support, we can overcome obstacles and stay motivated on our journey to unlock the secrets to optimal sleep and performance.

Strategies for sustaining healthy sleep habits in the long term

In today's fast-paced world, it's easy to overlook the importance of a good night's sleep. Many people sacrifice quality sleep in favor of work, socializing, or other activities. However, the power of sleep cannot be underestimated. It is essential for optimal performance, overall health, and well-being. In this subchapter, we will explore strategies for sustaining healthy sleep habits in the long term.

1. Establish a consistent sleep schedule: Our bodies thrive on routine. Going to bed and waking up at the same time every day can help regulate our internal clock and improve sleep quality. Aim for a minimum of seven to eight hours of sleep each night.

2. Create a sleep-friendly environment: Make your bedroom a sanctuary for sleep. Ensure the room is dark, quiet, and at a comfortable temperature. Remove electronic devices that emit blue light, such as smartphones and tablets, as they can interfere with sleep patterns.

3. Practice relaxation techniques: Incorporate relaxation techniques into your bedtime routine. Deep breathing exercises, meditation, or gentle stretching can help calm the mind and prepare the body for sleep. Avoid stimulating activities or stressful situations close to bedtime.

4. Limit exposure to electronic devices: The blue light emitted by electronic devices can disrupt the production of melatonin, a hormone that regulates sleep. To promote healthy sleep habits, avoid using electronic devices at least one hour before bed. Instead, engage in relaxing activities such as reading a book or taking a warm bath.

5. Manage stress levels: High levels of stress can negatively impact sleep quality. Find healthy ways to manage stress, such as practicing mindfulness, exercising regularly, or seeking support from friends and family. Consider incorporating stress-reducing activities into your daily routine.

6. Avoid stimulants: Caffeine, nicotine, and alcohol can interfere with sleep patterns. Limit your consumption of these substances, especially in the evening. Opt for herbal tea or decaffeinated beverages instead.

7. Prioritize regular exercise: Engaging in regular physical activity can improve sleep quality. Aim for at least 30 minutes of moderate exercise most days of the week. However, avoid exercising too close to bedtime, as it may increase alertness and make it harder to fall asleep.

By implementing these strategies, you can develop and sustain healthy sleep habits in the long term. Remember, sleep is not a luxury but a necessity. By prioritizing your sleep, you can unlock the secrets to optimal sleep and performance, leading to a happier, healthier, and more productive life.

Seeking support and accountability for continued success

In our quest for optimal sleep and performance, it is essential to recognize the value of seeking support and accountability. While it may seem tempting to go at it alone, the reality is that we can achieve far greater success when we have a network of individuals who understand and support our goals.

One of the first steps in seeking support is to identify those who can play a positive role in our journey. This could include friends, family members, or even colleagues who share similar aspirations for improving their sleep and overall well-being. By reaching out to these individuals, we create a support system that can offer encouragement, advice, and motivation when we need it most.

Accountability is another crucial aspect of our quest for continued success. When we commit to making positive changes in our sleep habits, it is essential to hold ourselves accountable for following through on these commitments. One way to do this is by setting clear goals and tracking our progress. This could involve using a sleep journal to record our sleep patterns, implementing a bedtime routine, or even utilizing sleep-tracking devices to monitor our sleep quality. By regularly reviewing our progress, we can identify areas for improvement and stay motivated to achieve our goals.

In addition to personal accountability, seeking external accountability can also be highly effective. This could involve finding an accountability partner or joining a sleep support group where sedividuals can share their experiences, challenges, and successes. These platforms provide a space for open dialogue, allowing us to learn from others, gain new insights, and stay on track with our sleep goals.

It is important to remember that seeking support and accountability is not a sign of weakness but rather a sign of strength. By acknowledging that we cannot do it all on our own, we are taking an active step towards our own success. We all face obstacles and setbacks on our journey to optimal sleep and performance, but with the support and accountability of others, we can navigate these challenges more effectively and achieve our desired outcomes.

In conclusion, seeking support and accountability is a vital component of our quest for continued success in improving our sleep habits. By surrounding ourselves with individuals who understand and support our goals, and by holding ourselves accountable for our actions, we can make significant progress towards unlocking the secrets to optimal sleep and performance. Remember, we are not alone in this journey, and together, we can achieve greatness.

Chapter 6: Conclusion: Embracing the Power of Sleep

Recap of Key Concepts and Takeaways

In the previous chapters of "Sleep Smarter: Unlocking the Secrets to Optimal Sleep and Performance," we have delved into the power of sleep and its impact on our overall well-being and performance. As we wrap up this book, it's crucial to recap the key concepts and takeaways that can help us harness the full potential of restful sleep.

First and foremost, we have learned that sleep is not a luxury but a necessity. It is during sleep that our bodies undergo crucial restorative processes, repairing tissues, consolidating memories, and regulating hormones. Without sufficient sleep, we put ourselves at risk of numerous health issues, including obesity, diabetes, heart disease, and even mental health disorders.

One of the key takeaways from this book is the importance of establishing a consistent sleep routine. Going to bed and waking up at the same time each day helps regulate our internal body clock, known as the circadian rhythm. By aligning our sleep-wake cycle with this natural rhythm, we can optimize the quality and duration of our sleep.

Another concept we explored is the role of our sleep environment. Creating a sleep-friendly environment involves ensuring a cool, dark, and quiet room, free from electronic devices and distractions. Implementing relaxation techniques such as deep breathing, meditation, and aromatherapy can also help calm the mind and prepare the body for sleep.

We also discussed the significance of optimizing our sleep quality through proper nutrition and exercise. Consuming a balanced diet, rich in sleep-promoting nutrients like magnesium, tryptophan, and vitamin B6, can positively impact our sleep patterns. Regular physical activity, particularly in the morning or early afternoon, can enhance our sleep quality by reducing stress and promoting relaxation.

Lastly, we emphasized the detrimental effects of blue light exposure from electronic devices, particularly before bedtime. The blue light emitted by screens disrupts our natural melatonin production, making it harder for us to fall asleep. Implementing a digital curfew and utilizing blue light-blocking glasses can mitigate this issue and promote better sleep hygiene.

By understanding the power of sleep and implementing the strategies discussed in this book, we can unlock our full potential in various aspects of life. From improved cognitive function and productivity to enhanced physical performance and overall well-being, prioritizing sleep is key.

Remember, sleep is not a luxury; it is an essential pillar of optimal health and performance. Let us embrace the power of sleep and make it a non-negotiable part of our daily routine to live a healthier, happier, and more productive life.

Summarizing the importance of optimal sleep

Subchapter: Summarizing the Importance of Optimal Sleep

Introduction:
In today's fast-paced world, sleep often takes a backseat to our busy schedules. However, it is crucial to understand the significance of optimal sleep for our overall well-being and performance. This subchapter aims to summarize the importance of sleep, shedding light on its power and the benefits it brings to our lives.

The   Power   of   Sleep:
Sleep is not just a time to rest; it is a critical period during which our bodies rejuvenate, repair, and recharge. Optimal sleep ensures better cognitive function, emotional stability, and physical health. It plays a pivotal role in our performance, productivity, and overall quality of life.

Enhanced   Brain   Function:
Quality sleep is essential for optimal brain function. During sleep, the brain consolidates memories, enhances learning, and improves problem-solving skills. Lack of sleep can impair cognitive abilities, such as memory retention, decision-making, and creativity. By prioritizing sleep, we can enhance our mental clarity, focus, and overall cognitive performance.

Improved   Emotional   Well-being:
Sleep deprivation can lead to heightened emotional reactivity, mood swings, and even mental health issues like anxiety and depression. Optimal sleep promotes emotional stability, stress reduction, and a better ability to manage emotions. By ensuring enough sleep, we can enhance our emotional well-being and foster healthier relationships.

Physical Health and Vitality: Sleep is closely linked to our physical health. Adequate sleep supports a stronger immune system, reduces the risk of chronic diseases like heart disease, diabetes, and obesity, and boosts overall vitality. It plays a crucial role in maintaining a healthy weight, improving athletic performance, and accelerating post-workout recovery.

Boosted Performance and Productivity: Sleep is a fundamental aspect of peak performance. By optimizing our sleep, we can increase productivity, creativity, and problem-solving abilities. Lack of sleep, on the other hand, leads to decreased focus, attention, and overall performance. Prioritizing sleep allows us to maximize our potential and excel in our personal and professional lives.

Conclusion:

In conclusion, optimal sleep is not a luxury but a necessity for a fulfilling and successful life. Understanding the power of sleep and its impact on our cognitive function, emotional well-being, physical health, and overall performance is the first step towards prioritizing it. By making a conscious effort to get enough quality sleep, we can unlock the secrets to optimal sleep and unleash our true potential. Remember, sleep smarter, live better!

Highlighting the strategies and techniques discussed

In the subchapter titled "Highlighting the strategies and techniques discussed," the book "Sleep Smarter: Unlocking the Secrets to Optimal Sleep and Performance" brings together a comprehensive set of strategies and techniques to harness the incredible power of sleep. This section serves as a summary of the key takeaway points and highlights the transformative benefits that can be achieved by implementing these strategies.

One of the primary strategies emphasized in this book is the establishment of a consistent sleep schedule. By going to bed and waking up at the same time every day, our bodies can develop a natural sleep-wake cycle, optimizing the quality of our sleep and enhancing overall performance. Understanding the significance of circadian rhythms and their impact on our sleep patterns is essential for achieving optimal sleep.

Another important technique discussed is the creation of a sleep-conducive environment. This entails minimizing noise and distractions, controlling room temperature, and ensuring a comfortable mattress and pillow. By optimizing our sleeping environment, we can improve sleep quality and enhance our ability to fall asleep faster and stay asleep throughout the night.

The book also delves into the power of nutrition and its impact on sleep. Highlighting the importance of a balanced diet and specific nutrients, it explores how certain foods can promote better sleep. Incorporating foods rich in tryptophan, magnesium, and melatonin into our diet can help regulate our sleep patterns and improve sleep quality.

In addition to lifestyle factors, the book emphasizes the significance of relaxation techniques. Techniques such as meditation, deep breathing exercises, and mindfulness can help calm the mind and prepare the body for a restful sleep. By incorporating these practices into our bedtime routine, we can reduce stress levels and promote a sense of relaxation conducive to a good night's sleep.

Lastly, the book acknowledges the role of technology in our sleep patterns. It provides insights into the negative impact of electronic devices on sleep and offers strategies to minimize their effect. Establishing digital curfews, using blue light-blocking glasses, and creating technology-free zones in the bedroom are among the techniques suggested to optimize sleep in the digital age.

By implementing these strategies and techniques, readers can unlock the secrets to optimal sleep and performance. Whether aiming to enhance productivity, improve overall health, or simply enjoy a more rejuvenating sleep experience, "Sleep Smarter" offers practical solutions that can be applied by anyone seeking to harness the power of sleep in their lives.

Embracing a Sleep-First Mindset

In today's fast-paced world, it's all too common for sleep to take a backseat to our demanding schedules and endless to-do lists. However, if there's one thing we need to prioritize above all else, it's the quality and quantity of our sleep. In this subchapter, we will explore the concept of embracing a sleep-first mindset and uncover the powerful benefits that come with it.

A sleep-first mindset means recognizing that sleep is not a luxury but a necessity for our overall well-being and performance. It means understanding that by prioritizing our sleep, we can unlock our full potential and achieve optimal levels of health, productivity, and happiness.

One of the key secrets to embracing a sleep-first mindset is understanding the power of sleep. Sleep is not just a time for rest; it is a critical period during which our bodies and minds undergo essential processes for repair, growth, and restoration. When we prioritize sleep, we give our bodies the time and resources they need to heal, recharge, and function at their best.

Research has shown that a lack of sleep can have profound negative effects on our physical health, mental well-being, cognitive function, and overall performance. Chronic sleep deprivation has been linked to an increased risk of obesity, diabetes, heart disease, and even certain types of cancer. On the other hand, getting enough high-quality sleep can enhance our immune system, improve our memory and concentration, boost our mood, and increase our creativity and problem-solving abilities.

To truly embrace a sleep-first mindset, we need to make sleep a priority in our daily lives. This means establishing a consistent sleep schedule, creating a sleep-friendly environment, and adopting healthy sleep habits. It also involves recognizing and addressing any potential barriers to sleep, such as stress, technology, or poor sleep hygiene.

By prioritizing sleep and embracing a sleep-first mindset, we can transform our lives in profound ways. We can experience increased energy levels, improved physical and mental health, enhanced productivity, and a greater sense of well-being. Ultimately, by understanding and harnessing the power of sleep, we can unlock the secrets to optimal sleep and performance, leading to a healthier, happier, and more fulfilling life.

In conclusion, embracing a sleep-first mindset is crucial for anyone seeking to harness the power of sleep. By recognizing the importance of sleep and making it a priority in our lives, we can unlock the secrets to optimal sleep and performance. So, let's embrace this mindset and prioritize our sleep for a healthier, happier, and more successful life.

Shifting priorities and valuing sleep as a foundation for success

In today's fast-paced world, we often find ourselves juggling multiple responsibilities and constantly striving for success. However, in our pursuit of achievement, one crucial aspect that often gets overlooked is sleep. In this subchapter, we aim to shed light on the importance of shifting our priorities and valuing sleep as a foundation for success.

Sleep is not just a luxury or a time to rest; it is a powerful tool that can significantly impact our overall well-being and performance. The power of sleep lies in its ability to restore and rejuvenate our bodies, enhance cognitive function, and support emotional balance. By understanding this, we can begin to realize that quality sleep is not an option but a necessity for optimal functioning.

One of the key aspects discussed in this subchapter is the need to shift our priorities and make sleep a non-negotiable part of our daily routine. Many individuals tend to sacrifice sleep in favor of work or other activities, believing that it will lead to increased productivity. However, research has shown that chronic sleep deprivation can have detrimental effects on cognitive abilities, memory retention, decision-making skills, and overall productivity.

To truly harness the power of sleep, it is vital to prioritize it and create a sleep-friendly environment. This includes establishing a consistent sleep schedule, optimizing sleep environment conditions such as temperature and lighting, and implementing relaxation techniques to prepare the mind and body for quality rest.

Additionally, this subchapter delves into the concept of sleep hygiene, emphasizing the importance of adopting healthy habits that promote better sleep. These habits may include minimizing exposure to electronic devices before bedtime, avoiding caffeine and stimulants close to sleep hours, and engaging in relaxation techniques such as meditation or reading.

By valuing sleep as a foundation for success, we open ourselves up to a world of improved well-being and enhanced performance. Not only can quality sleep increase focus, creativity, and problem-solving abilities, but it can also positively impact our physical health, immune system, and emotional resilience.

In conclusion, this subchapter serves as a wake-up call for individuals across all niches to prioritize sleep and recognize its undeniable power. By shifting our priorities and adopting healthy sleep habits, we can unlock the secrets to optimal sleep and performance, leading us to a life of success, fulfillment, and overall well-being.

Recognizing the long-term benefits of investing in quality sleep

In a world that glorifies productivity and constantly demands our attention, we often overlook the importance of quality sleep. However, understanding the long-term benefits of investing in our sleep can be a game-changer for our overall health and performance. In this subchapter, we will delve into the power of sleep and why it should become a priority in our lives.

Sleep is not just a state of rest; it is a fundamental pillar of optimal performance. When we sleep, our bodies undergo a series of crucial processes that rejuvenate and repair our physical and mental well-being. From consolidating memories to regulating hormones, sleep plays a vital role in almost every aspect of our lives.

One of the most significant long-term benefits of quality sleep is its impact on cognitive function. Inadequate sleep not only impairs our focus and attention but also hinders our ability to learn and make decisions. On the other hand, getting enough sleep enhances our creativity, problem-solving skills, and memory retention. Investing in quality sleep can, therefore, lead to improved academic and professional performance, ultimately boosting our success in various areas of life.

Moreover, quality sleep is closely linked to our emotional well-being. Lack of sleep can leave us more vulnerable to stress, anxiety, and mood disorders. By prioritizing sleep, we can regulate our emotions more effectively, leading to better mental health and increased resilience in facing life's challenges.

In terms of physical health, investing in quality sleep has numerous long-term benefits. Studies have shown that chronic sleep deprivation increases the risk of developing obesity, diabetes, cardiovascular diseases, and even certain types of cancer. On the other hand, getting enough sleep promotes a healthy metabolism, regulates appetite, and strengthens the immune system. By recognizing the power of sleep, we can significantly improve our overall physical well-being and decrease the likelihood of facing such health issues in the future.

In conclusion, understanding the long-term benefits of investing in quality sleep is essential for everyone, regardless of their niche or occupation. By prioritizing sleep, we unlock the secrets to optimal performance and overall well-being. From improved cognitive function and emotional stability to enhanced physical health, sleep has the potential to transform our lives. It is time to recognize the power of sleep and make it a non-negotiable part of our daily routine.

Unlocking Your Potential through Optimal Sleep and Performance

Sleep is a critical aspect of our lives that often goes overlooked and undervalued. In today's fast-paced world, it's common to sacrifice sleep in order to meet the demands of work, family, and social obligations. However, this lack of sleep can have detrimental effects on our overall well-being and our ability to perform at our best.

In this subchapter, we will explore the power of sleep and how it can unlock your potential for optimal performance. We will delve into the secrets of achieving quality sleep and provide practical tips to help you improve your sleep habits.

Sleep is not merely a time of rest; it is a time of rejuvenation and restoration. During sleep, our bodies repair and regenerate, our minds consolidate memories and learning, and our immune system strengthens. Without adequate sleep, these essential processes are compromised, leading to decreased cognitive function, impaired decision-making, and increased susceptibility to illnesses.

To unlock your potential, it's crucial to prioritize sleep and create a conducive sleep environment. Start by establishing a consistent sleep schedule, going to bed and waking up at the same time every day. This helps regulate your internal body clock and enhances the quality of your sleep.

Additionally, optimize your sleep environment by making your bedroom a sanctuary for rest. Keep the room dark, quiet, and at a comfortable temperature. Invest in a supportive mattress and pillows that promote proper spinal alignment. Remove electronic devices from your bedroom and create a relaxing bedtime routine to signal your body that it's time to wind down.

Furthermore, pay attention to your sleep hygiene. Avoid stimulating activities, such as exercise and caffeine consumption, close to bedtime. Instead, engage in relaxing activities like reading or taking a warm bath. Minimize exposure to blue light from screens by using blue light filters or wearing blue light-blocking glasses.

By prioritizing sleep and implementing these strategies, you can unlock your full potential for optimal performance. Improved sleep quality will enhance your cognitive abilities, increase your productivity, and boost your overall well-being.

In conclusion, sleep is a powerful tool that can unlock your potential for optimal performance. By understanding the importance of sleep and implementing strategies to improve your sleep quality, you can maximize your potential in all areas of life. Take the necessary steps today to unlock your potential through optimal sleep and performance.

Inspiring readers to take action and make positive changes

In today's fast-paced world, it's easy to overlook the importance of quality sleep. We often prioritize work, socializing, and other responsibilities over getting enough rest. However, understanding the power of sleep and making positive changes in our sleep habits can have a profound impact on our overall well-being and performance.

Welcome to the subchapter on inspiring readers to take action and make positive changes in their sleep habits for optimal sleep and performance. In this section, we will explore the incredible benefits that come from prioritizing sleep, and how you can make simple yet effective changes to reap these rewards.

Sleep is not just a period of rest; it is a vital process that allows our bodies and minds to rejuvenate and repair themselves. By unlocking the secrets to optimal sleep, you will not only experience increased energy levels and improved cognitive function but also enjoy better physical health and emotional well-being.

We will delve into the power of sleep and how it affects various aspects of our lives, from productivity and creativity to weight management and overall happiness. By understanding these connections, you will be inspired to take action and make sleep a priority in your life.

This subchapter will provide you with practical tips and strategies to optimize your sleep routine. From creating a sleep-friendly environment to establishing a consistent sleep schedule, you will learn how to set yourself up for success and achieve the quality sleep your body and mind deserve.

Additionally, we will explore the importance of implementing relaxation techniques before bed and adopting healthy sleep habits to enhance your sleep quality. By incorporating these practices into your daily routine, you will be able to make positive changes that will transform the way you sleep and perform in all areas of your life.

Remember, it's never too late to prioritize sleep and make positive changes. By taking action and implementing the strategies discussed in this subchapter, you will unlock the secrets to optimal sleep and performance. Get ready to embark on a journey towards a healthier, more energized, and fulfilling life through the power of sleep.

In conclusion, this subchapter aims to inspire readers from all walks of life to take action and make positive changes in their sleep habits. By understanding the incredible benefits of quality sleep and implementing practical strategies, you will unlock the secrets to optimal sleep and performance. Get ready to transform your life by harnessing the power of sleep!

Encouraging the pursuit of optimal sleep for improved performance in all areas of life.

Encouraging the Pursuit of Optimal Sleep for Improved Performance in All Areas of Life

In today's fast-paced world, sleep is often overlooked as a crucial component of our overall well-being. We live in a society that glorifies late nights, early mornings, and burning the candle at both ends. However, research has shown time and again that optimal sleep is essential for improved performance in all areas of life. In this subchapter, we will explore the power of sleep and how prioritizing it can unlock our full potential.

Sleep is not just a time of rest; it is a vital period of rejuvenation and repair for both our bodies and minds. During sleep, our brain processes information, consolidates memories, and restores cognitive function. Without sufficient sleep, our attention span, creativity, and problem-solving abilities suffer. By prioritizing optimal sleep, we can enhance our cognitive performance, making us more effective in our personal and professional lives.

Beyond cognitive performance, sleep also plays a significant role in our physical health. Lack of sleep has been linked to a wide range of health issues, including obesity, diabetes, and cardiovascular disease. On the other hand, getting enough sleep can boost our immune system, regulate our hormones, and improve our energy levels. By embracing optimal sleep habits, we can enhance our physical health and overall well-being.

Furthermore, sleep has a profound impact on our emotional well-being. Sleep deprivation can lead to heightened stress, anxiety, and mood swings. On the contrary, a good night's sleep can improve our emotional resilience, regulate our emotions, and enhance our overall mental health. By prioritizing optimal sleep, we can foster emotional stability and improve our relationships with others.

To encourage the pursuit of optimal sleep, it is crucial to establish healthy sleep habits. This includes maintaining a consistent sleep schedule, creating a sleep-friendly environment, and practicing relaxation techniques before bed. This subchapter will provide practical tips and strategies to help anyone achieve the optimal sleep they need for improved performance in all areas of life.

In conclusion, sleep is not a luxury but a necessity for optimal performance in all areas of our lives. By recognizing the power of sleep and prioritizing it, we can unlock our full potential. Whether you are a student, a professional, or a homemaker, embracing optimal sleep habits will enhance your cognitive performance, physical health, and emotional well-being. So, let's prioritize sleep and reap the benefits it offers for a better and more fulfilling life.